LAW AND THE FAMILY

About the Author

Maureen Mullally is a practising barrister who has specialised in family law for twenty years. She is a member of the English and Irish Bar and of the Family Law Bar Association.

LAW AND THE FAMILY

A PRACTICAL GUIDE

2nd EDITION

Maureen Mullally LL.B.

BLACKHALL *Publishing*

First published in 1994 in the UK by Hodder & Stoughton Ltd

This edition was typeset by
Gough Typesetting Services for
BLACKHALL PUBLISHING
26 Eustace Street,
Dublin 2
Ireland
(e-mail: blackhall@tinet.ie)

ISBN: 1 901657 53 1

A catalogue record for this book is
available from the British Library.

Printed in Ireland by
Colourbooks.

AUTHOR'S NOTE

All the case studies in this book are completely fictional. They illustrate what might happen in certain circumstances and they have been deliberately simplified. Real life cases are usually, infinitely more complicated – and no two cases have identical facts! So please do not compare the facts of your case with any of mine in the belief that it will tell you exactly what result you can expect.

Although every effort has been made to ensure that all information given is accurate at the time of going to press, this is not a legal textbook and is not intended to replace professional advice in cases of any difficulty.

Legal Disclaimer

ACKNOWLEDGEMENTS

I would like to acknowledge the help advice and encouragement which I have had from so many friends and colleagues and in particular Dame Margaret Booth, who inspired in me during my pupillage her own enthusiasm for family law; Mary Rose Mullally, my solicitor daughter, who read the manuscript and made constructive comments; my husband John and my Clerks, both at Lamb Building and Westgate Chambers, without whose forbearance the second edition would never have been finished, and the team at Blackhall Publishing who have given such invaluable editorial guidance.

Maureen Mullally
April 1999

To my dear John who shares my family and encourages my law.

CONTENTS

Section IV: Families In Crisis

Section V: Practicalities

FOREWORD

to the first edition

by Helena Kennedy QC

Maureen Mullally's book is that joyful experience: a book about the law which is accessible, informative and easy to read. It penetrates some of the dark recesses of the legal system, which can seem so unfathomable to the very people whom the law is supposed to serve.

Knowing about the law and being able to use it should be the entitlement of every citizen in Britain but, unfortunately, we still shroud the law in too much mystique, with lawyers often using language which excludes understanding and confuses rather than clarifies.

However, the general public is now better informed, generally, and more demanding of its professionals than ever before. People are no longer prepared to accept the paternalism of the past, which meant being patted on the back and told to leave their case to the experts. They want to be involved in a collaborative process and to embark on any legal journey with a clear understanding of what is involved. Without knowledge, how can we make the most important decisions of our lives?

One of the great challenges to any legal system is that it keeps in tune with the changing world. The 20th century has seen considerable changes in the status of women, which has inevitably led to a renegotiation of relationships between the sexes. People's expectations of marriage are now different and divorce has greatly increased. Childrearing methods have developed, with a greater appreciation of children's needs and a growing emphasis on children's rights and parental responsibility. This period is undoubtedly one of transition with painful consequences for many couples and it is to the courts that they invariably turn for resolution of conflict.

Ready access to the law is a fundamental right in any democracy but it can be meaningless if the process is prohibitively costly and the procedure frighteningly obscure. The battle for wider legal aid provision will have to be confronted in other ways but informative guides like this can provide much-needed knowledge to the non-lawyer.

Families, albeit in greater variety than in previous generations, remain a fundamental part of our social arrangements, crucial to our individual and national well-being, often determining who we are and how we relate to the world. They can be a source of stability and nurturance, havens of security and love, but not always. Misty-eyed portrayals of the good, old-fashioned family often deny the reality with which the courts have to deal. As Maureen Mullally so lucidly explains, abuses formerly veiled in secrecy, such as incest and domestic violence, are now being openly disclosed. Solutions to such profound social problems cannot rest entirely with the courts but the law has a powerful role in issuing messages which reverberate throughout society.

I know that *Law and the Family* will be an invaluable resource for anyone embarking upon a case in the family courts or anyone wanting a general understanding of family law. The author is a fine lawyer who illuminates her subject with humanity and compassion. For me this book is testimony that light can be shone on the law to the benefit of us all.

Helena Kennedy QC
1994

INTRODUCTION

Why this Book?

Every day of the week, in family courts in every town and county, men, women and children come face to face with the law. You are probably reading this book because the law is affecting, or is going to affect, you and your family in some way soon. Perhaps your marriage has broken down, maybe you can't decide which one of you the children will live with or you are trapped in a violent relationship. Whatever your reason for coming into contact with the law, it will no doubt be an emotional and stressful time, a time when the last thing you want to contemplate is being involved in legal proceedings.

To many people, the law can seem very intimidating and the mental image which people have of courts and lawyers is no help. Television and film scenes leave viewers with the impression that court proceedings are conducted in an atmosphere of high drama, with witnesses being unmercifully and sarcastically bullied by ruthless and overbearing cross examination. My own husband has always refused to come to see me in court. He says that he has one idea of me and does not want it changed!

The legal jargon alone might leave you feeling completely baffled. You might get into court to find judges and barristers, wigged and gowned like creatures from some other world, speaking what sounds to you like pure gobbledegook, while you are thinking, "Hang on a minute, please. Use words that I can understand. After all, this is my life you're talking about."

Well, the good news is that things are not quite like that in family courts. In the first place, it is very unlikely that you will see wigs and gowns. Most cases which have to do with the family are heard in courts which are not open to the public. No one can come into court who is not directly concerned with the case. The judges and other lawyers do not wear their wigs and gowns when the court is closed to the public. There will be a sign outside the court which says "Court in Chambers" and that simply means "Keep out unless this is *your* case".

What has happened to Family Law?

Over the past twenty years or so there has been a dramatic change in family law. In our grandparents' day, family life was an intensely private business. Marriages, births and deaths had to be registered. Apart from that, unless a crime had been committed, the law left the family strictly alone.

For countless generations, the "family" meant the husband and wife living together until one of them died, bringing up their children, sticking to one another through good times and bad. Nobody moved too far away from where they were born. So brothers and sisters of the partners, grandparents, uncles, aunts and cousins would all be part of normal family life, with everyone supporting each other in their own marriages. Until fairly recently it was unusual for a man and a woman to live together as husband and wife, having a sexual relationship and bringing up children, without going through a ceremony of marriage. Single parent families were only likely to occur when one partner had been widowed. The shame attached to the idea of illegitimacy meant that unmarried mothers were usually forced to give up their babies.

But changes in the structure of the family have meant that the law has had to become more involved in family matters. Many young people leave their home area to work or study considerable distances away. They marry, or start relationships, and make new homes far from their families. Cut off from family support by distance, couples tend to find themselves a bit isolated in times of difficulty or trouble. This is a factor which has played its part in increasing the breakdown of relationships and led to a greater acceptance of divorce and single-parenting.

Over recent years, there have been many laws passed which deal with the family and there has been a totally new approach to family law. The aim has been to get rid of formality and bewildering legal language as far as humanly possible. Family lawyers, whether they are judges, barristers, or solicitors, are keen to make sure that people know exactly what is going on and how what is going on is likely to affect them.

How this Book will Help you

If you are not legally qualified you may, find it difficult to know how to set about things when it comes to a legal matter which affects you or your family. For example, what is the first step? Where can you go for advice? Can the law actually, help you with your family problem? When you come to court, what can you expect? In this book, you will find explanations of many of the most common ways in which law can affect the family on a day-to-day basis, together with suggestions about how you might want to proceed or people you might want to contact. At the end of some chapters there is a list of addresses which may be useful. This is not a legal textbook and I have tried to avoid legal language as far as I can, but it is obviously not always possible to avoid using legal terms and you are bound to come across unfamiliar words. So at the end of the book you will find a glossary of legal terms, giving simple explanations of what they mean. The book is divided into five sections, so that you can quickly find the topic you may be looking for.

Scottish Law

Scotland has its own laws, and in its family and divorce laws and procedures are not the same as those for England and Wales. However, the child support law covers Scotland as well as England and Wales.

SECTION I

COUPLES

CHAPTER ONE

ARE YOU SPLITTING UP?

What Used to Happen

In 1936, Edward VIII, already the King of England, was faced with an impossible choice. He had fallen deeply in love with Wallis Simpson. She was an American, which would have been quite bad enough, but even worse was the fact that she had been divorced. The King desperately hoped that he would be able to marry her and, at the same time, keep his crown, but it was made quite clear to him by his advisers that he could not possibly have both the kingship and the woman he loved. This was in spite of his great popularity with the people. However popular he was, it was simply not possible for him to marry someone who had been divorced. He made his choice, and gave up his throne in favour of his brother, the father of Queen Elizabeth II. Edward VIII became the Duke of Windsor, married Wallis and lived in exile from his own country for the rest of his life. Sometimes it seems hard to believe that all this happened less than 60 years ago.

In the early 1950s Princess Margaret, sister of Queen Elizabeth, fell in love with Group Captain Townsend. He was in many ways a suitable match for a princess, having had a distinguished wartime service career, followed by a stint serving as one of Buckingham Palace's most trusted courtiers. But he also had been divorced. Princess Margaret too was faced with a stark choice. She chose her duty, and she and the Group Captain had to part.

When you contrast those two pieces of history with the present day, you realise how our attitudes to divorce have changed over a few short decades. Princess Margaret herself was divorced from her husband in 1978. Three out of the Queen's four children have been through the heartbreak and trauma of marital breakdown. Sadly none of this is very unusual as one in every three marriages now ends in divorce.

But, perhaps rather surprisingly, the high rate of marriage break-down does not seem to be discouraging people. Now more than a third of all marriages celebrated are marriages where the husband, the wife, or both partners, are having another shot at marital bliss. And some of those husbands and wives are trying for the third, fourth or even fifth time!

It is difficult to say why so many marriages are breaking down today. When most people were committed to a religion and attended a church regularly their marriages were bolstered by their faith. Marriage was a sacrament, an undertaking until death intervened.

Only the church had any power over marriage in those days. Divorce was a possibility but quite rare. In the time of Henry VIII a divorce could be obtained, as Henry's well-known exploits demonstrate, but a divorce was certainly not an option for anyone but the extremely rich and influential. Henry wanted to divorce his first queen, so that he could marry the fascinating Anne Boleyn, partly because he had fallen in love with Anne but also partly because he had no son and heir, and hoped that Anne would be able to produce one for him.

The problem for Henry was that only the Pope in Rome could grant a divorce. The Pope, for reasons not unconnected with European politics, was not prepared to help Henry with his plan. Henry, in a temper, declared himself head of the Church in England and granted himself his own divorce. Even for hundreds of years after that, a divorce could only be had through the Church Courts at enormous expense and as a result of a very slow process.

No doubt some marriages were unhappy, but most people had very little expectation of married happiness in those days. Marriages were usually arranged between the families of the bride and groom with the young people themselves having had very little say in the arrangements. Remarriage was fairly common, and that was because people generally had a much shorter life span. Childbirth was a risky business and many mothers simply did not survive it. Medicine was in its infancy and most diseases were just incurable. As a result, a husband or wife lucky enough to enjoy good health might outlive several spouses and remarry several times.

Most of us live much longer today. It is not all that unusual for happily married couples to live to celebrate their golden and even their diamond wedding anniversaries. For those lucky enough to have found happiness, these are real occasions for celebrating. But for unhappily married people, the prospect of 60 years of togetherness can sound more like a life sentence.

Even when divorce had become something which the civil courts decided, rather than a matter for the church, a husband and a wife did not come to the court on anything like equal terms. First, the husband was usually the one with the money, so that he would have been the one who was able to afford to try for a divorce. But even when a wife could afford to try to get a divorce, she was treated differently. A husband could get a divorce simply on the ground that his wife had committed adultery. But if a wife wanted a divorce because of her husband's adultery she had to prove that the adultery had been incestuous, or had been coupled with bigamy, rape, sodomy, bestiality or cruelty.

If a woman who had children was found to have committed adultery, she could say goodbye to the children forever, no matter how young they were. But a father who had committed adultery would not have had to suffer separation from his children. Children belonged to their fathers, who could do pretty much as they pleased with them.

If you were asking for a divorce and you had committed adultery yourself you might be refused the divorce. If you were a divorced person you were someone to be avoided, especially if you happened to be a woman. The person who had been divorced was particularly shunned as being the 'guilty' party.

Irretrievable Breakdown

In 1969, an attempt was made to get rid of the idea that there had to be a guilty party in every divorce case. It was decided that the only ground for a divorce should be the irretrievable breakdown of the marriage – in other words that there could only be a divorce in cases where there was no hope whatsoever of the marriage surviving. But unfortunately parliament then went on to decide that the breakdown had to be shown in one of five ways. The ways in which breakdown could be shown were to be adultery, unreasonable behaviour, desertion for two years, living apart for two years if both partners agreed to a divorce, and living apart for five years, even if one of the partners did not want a divorce.

To be accused of committing adultery, or of behaving so unreasonably that someone should not be expected to live with you have, not surprisingly, continued to inflame emotions. Going through a divorce is still one of the most stressful experiences which anyone can have, and being branded as the guilty party just makes matters worse. The truth is that in far and away the majority of divorces there is no guilty party and no innocent party. Marriages break down for all sorts of reasons, but it usually takes two to break a marriage just as it takes two to make one successful.

If we could get rid of the notions of guilt and innocence in marriage breakdown, it could help lessen the grief and bitterness which most divorcing couples experience. Even more importantly, it could relieve some of the desperate unhappiness experienced by the countless numbers of children unlucky enough to be caught up in the crossfire between warring parents.

Divorce and Legal Separation Today

Today one in every three marriages in this country ends in breakdown. If you are involved in a divorce yourself, or if you have been, you will know that behind this bland statistic is hidden an unimaginable amount of human misery. People who go through marriage breakdown feel disappointment, anger, bitterness, grief, rejection and inadequacy. On top of all that, there is the sense of utter loneliness and isolation. After all, you have invested your whole self in this relationship. Whatever it is that has gone wrong, your self confidence must have taken quite a knock. The grief is very similar to that of bereavement by death. This is not surprising, for the death of a relationship is often just as shattering as the loss of a close friend or family member.

Unfortunately, when there are children of the marriage, they are likely to suffer even more than their parents. Adults can try to make sense of what has happened, to find explanations, children only know that their world has suddenly come to an end, when the two people who mean security and love to them decide that they no longer love one another. There is no way that a young child can possibly grasp the issues involved in marital breakdown. All he or she knows is that happiness has been destroyed. Child psychiatrists have discovered that children often blame themselves when their parents split up. To an adult that may seem laughable, but the effect on a child can be lifelong.

Why do so many Marriages Break Up Today?

No one really knows why so many marriages break up. Some experts think that young people are simply not being given enough proper preparation for adult relationships, including marriage. It may be that we should be concentrating more on training for adult relationships in schools, where the mechanics of sex education are often taught in complete isolation from other aspects of relating to other people which are just as important. We wouldn't dream of teaching little children to drive cars without explaining to them how dangerous a car can be if it is not properly controlled. Yet some teachers are quite happy to instruct their charges on the 'facts of life' without explaining that a sexual relationship can only result in unhappiness if the two people concerned have no love for or commitment towards one another.

No relationship between two people is ever going to be completely without problems. But 'it's the bad times that make the good times', as the Irish expression has it. Every couple lucky enough to have enjoyed a lasting relationship can look back over their years together and identify bad times, when the going got really rough, and one or both partners might have felt like giving it all up. But the fact that they did get through those times together will mean that their relationship has grown in strength as a result.

When things go wrong, divorce sometimes seems to be the easy solution. It may well be that our law has gone too far in making it such an easy option. When the divorce laws were reformed in the 1960s, nobody really expected that the divorce rate would rise as spectacularly as it has. It was thought that there might be an increase in divorce figures immediately, because many couples had been trapped for years in loveless unions from which there was no escape.

But after an initial rise in divorce figures, it was forecast that the divorce rate would settle down. Sadly, the annual numbers of divorces have been increasing ever since.

A solicitor, acting for someone who was filing a petition for divorce, had to give a certificate which said whether or not the possibility of a reconciliation had been discussed with the client before the petition was filed. The idea was to ensure that reconciliation had always been raised as a possibility before the divorce was applied for. It was hoped that this might prevent a couple rushing into a divorce without thinking matters through properly.

But solicitors would almost always file certificates which stated that the possibility of a reconciliation had not been discussed with the client. Solicitors are busy people. They do not generally see themselves as counsellors or marriage guidance experts. They might think that by the time someone had arrived at their offices to ask about getting a divorce it was probably far too late to start talking about reconciliation. That may, sometimes, be right. But it is a great pity that so many divorces went through without any attempt being made to see whether there is some other way to get round the problems in the marriage. This was obviously particularly true when there are any children, whose lives were going to be so shattered if there were to be a divorce.

Help with Problems

It is in an effort to remedy this that the new divorce law places much emphasis on the requirement that couples contemplating divorce will have to attend information sessions about the effects of the process. It is intended, when the new law comes into force, that help and advice will be offered to every couple in the hope that some marriages may be saved. Even for marriages where there is no hope, mediation sessions will be aimed at helping the partners reach agreement about the future for their children and about their finances, in the hope that some of the bitterness of the divorce experience may be avoided.

But even before the new law comes into force, anyone thinking about a divorce should first consider whether there is any possibility that expert counselling might be able to help. No matter how black things may look to you, it may well be that there is a way to save your relationship. You meant enough to one another to make the enormous commitment of getting married, maybe the even more important commitment of having children together; it is at least possible that you might be able to find that closeness again.

The first thing to realise is that the marriage in which there have never been problems is something which does not exist. It is not an admission of failure if you are having difficulties. But if things are going wrong you are likely to feel confused and unhappy, uncertain about what will be the right thing to do.

Help is at hand. Relate, which used to be called the Marriage Guidance Council, provides the principal counselling service for people having problems with relationships. Relate has about 400 centres throughout the country and over 50 years of experience in helping couples in trouble. Relate offers counselling to couples whether they are married or unmarried.

People are often worried by the idea of asking for counselling for their marriage. They wonder what the counsellors will be like. They may be put off by the idea that an interview with a counsellor will be like being summoned to the headmaster's study at school. They wonder if they will be treated as though they were neurotic or highly strung or stupid.

Relate counsellors are carefully selected and then trained for two years. Their training teaches them what makes relationships work – and what works against good relationships. They do not adopt a superior attitude. They do not 'tell people off', act as judges or preach. Unshockable, they are trained above all to listen.

The atmosphere at Relate centres is as relaxed and friendly as possible, with paper hankies at the ready. The problems people bring to the counsellors are as varied as the people themselves – inability to talk to a partner or to persuade a partner to talk to them perhaps, loneliness, jealousy, problems with children or in-laws. All these are just some examples of common difficulties.

Relate emphasise that the time to come for counselling, if possible, is when problems first arise. Waiting for them to resolve themselves may mean that by the time counselling is sought it is really too late because things have got themselves into such a terrible mess.

But that does not mean that counselling can never help when problems have existed for a long time. People can be helped at any stage.

The address and telephone number of the national headquarters of Relate are listed at the end of this chapter. Your local telephone directory should have the number of your local Relate centre where you can make an appointment for an initial interview. At that interview the counsellor will discuss the best kind of help for you. It night be that one, two or three sessions will be necessary to help. You might need more.

Obviously if both you and your partner go together, counselling is likely to be more successful. But even if your partner refuses to go, counselling can often help. If things do begin to improve between you as a result of the counselling sessions, your partner might be persuaded to come with you.

What the counsellor does during the sessions is to try to help you to understand your relationship, the problems which have come up, the possible causes for them, and the various choices available to you as solutions. The counsellor then helps you to work out your own answers to the problems. He or she does not tell you what to do. It is for you to consider the options open to you and to choose the one which seems best.

Mediation

Counsellors will not try to persuade you to stay together. They know how damaging a divorce can be, especially when there are children in the family, but they are realistic. They recognise that there is no hope for some relationships. If a marriage must end, the counsellor is trained to help the couple to separate with less anger or bitterness and to reach a fair and friendly settlement of matters concerning their children and any property which they own.

If you decide to go ahead with a divorce, you will obviously hope to minimise feelings of anger and bitterness in any areas where there might be disputes between you, over with whom the children should live, or what should happen to your home, for example. Counsellors are trained in mediation skills and can help separating partners to decide together what will be the best solution to problems about their children or money, or property matters. As they are completely, independent, no one need feel that a counsellor is 'on the other person's side'.

In addition to Relate, counselling is provided by such organisations as Marriage Care (formerly the Catholic Marriage Advisory Council) and the Jewish Marriage Council. You will find a list of addresses and telephone numbers at the end of this chapter.

Lawyers may not always seem the most helpful people when two people are splitting up; they do have a reputation for raising the temperature in divorce cases, However, this reputation is not entirely deserved. There are some lawyers who most certainly do write letters and conduct cases in a way which can only aggravate already explosive situations. But the majority of lawyers who specialise in family law are dedicated to keeping acrimony out of family disputes as far as they possibly can.

All committed family lawyers try to help people to reach sensible agreements rather than having court battles, if at all possible. The Family Mediators Association trains solicitors, barristers and other suitably qualified professionals in mediation techniques to enable them to help partners to come to agreements in areas of dispute.

Mediation is not an attempt to persuade parties to have a reconciliation. It accepts that there will be a divorce and simply concentrates on helping people to reach sensible agreements.

How to get a Divorce until the Law Changes

If you have been forced to the conclusion that there is no hope for your marriage, and you want to be divorced, it is not all that difficult to do it all yourself. But, if you need to sort out the arrangements about the children or property, it will probably be necessary to go to a solicitor.

The procedure for obtaining a divorce has been changed by parliament. The new procedure is being tested in some areas of the United Kingdom, but is not expected to come into general effect until the year 2000. In the meantime the old procedure still applies.

A series of helpful leaflets about divorce have been published by the Lord Chancellor's Department. Copies of the leaflets can be obtained at your local County Court or Citizen's Advice Bureau (addresses in the telephone book).

First, you must fill in a form called a 'petition'. These forms are free and can be obtained from your local County Court. The Court staff should be friendly and helpful, but they are not lawyers and cannot give legal advice on any questions you might have about the petition. You can start the divorce process in any divorce County Court or in the Principal Registry of the Family Division of the High Court.

You cannot petition for a divorce unless you have been married for more than one year. Once you have issued a petition you will be called 'the petitioner' by the Court and your husband or wife will be called 'the respondent'.

You, or your husband or wife, must be living permanently in England or Wales on the date when the petition is started, or one of you must have been living in England or Wales for at least a year on the day the petition is filed (i.e. left at the counter).

You will need:

(a) your own full name and address;

(b) your husband or wife's full name and address;

(c) a certified copy of your marriage certificate – please note that a photocopy will not do;

(d) names and dates of birth of any living children you have, even if they are over eighteen;

(e) if you are petitioning on adultery, and wish to name the person with whom the adultery was committed, that person's name and address.

If I have Lost my Marriage Certificate, what can I do?

If you were married in England or Wales, you can get a certified copy of your marriage certificate from whichever of the following is most convenient to you.

1. The office of the Registrar of Births, Deaths and Marriages for the district in which you were married. You can get the address

from the telephone directory. You will have to pay a fee; they will tell you how much it is.

2. The Registrar General
   ONS Southport
   Smedley Hydro
   Trafalgar Road
   Birkdale
   Southport PR8 2HH
   Tel: 0151 471 4200

   You cannot call in to this office. You can only apply by post and you must send a cheque or postal order for the correct amount. Cheques should be payable to 'HM Paymaster General'.

3. You can call in to the office at the:
   Office for National Statistics
   Family Records Centre
   1 Middleton Street
   London EC1R 1UW

   You will have to pay a fee for your copy certificate. The staff at the office will tell you how much it is.

The office you go to will want to know:

(a) the date and place of your marriage;

(b) your full name;

(c) the full name of your husband or wife.

Will I have to Pay a Fee to File a Petition?

You may have to pay a fee. The Court staff will be able to tell you how much it is. You may not have to pay if you are receiving:

(a) income support; or

(b) income-based job seekers allowance; or

(c) family credit; or

(d) disability working allowance; or

(e) solicitor's advice under the Legal Advice and Assistance Scheme [the 'Green Form Scheme']; or

(f) you receive another state benefit; or

(g) paying the fee would cause you undue hardship because of some exceptional circumstances in your case.

If you are in any of these situations, you can get a form from the Court on which you can apply to be exempted from payment of fees.

If everything is straightforward, you will not need to go to a solicitor. But you may have to consult a solicitor if you are not sure whether you have grounds for a divorce. These will be explained below.

You might have to go to a solicitor if, for example, your husband or wife is not likely to agree to the divorce, or if you have not been able to agree about who the children should live with, or how often they should see the parent with whom they are not living. Again, if there are going to be arguments about property or money, you may have to go for some legal advice.

Legal Aid

If you are eligible for legal aid, it does not automatically mean that all your legal fees will be met by the legal aid fund. If, for example, you decide to ask the court to make an order for financial support or about the matrimonial home or about some question relating to your children, you may find at the end of the day that you will have to pay back all the cost of the legal proceedings to the legal aid fund. This will happen if you get a lump sum or an interest in property as a result of the proceedings. For more information about legal costs see Chapter 16.

Grounds for Divorce

The law has been changed by parliament, so that, in the future, it will not be necessary to have a 'ground' for divorce. At present the new procedure is being tested in certain areas of the country. The new procedure is expected to come into force in the year 2000. Until then most divorces will be brought under the old procedure. Staff at your local County Court will be able to tell you whether you live in one of the areas where the new procedure is being tried out. If you do they will be able to tell you what to do. Otherwise the old procedure has to be followed for the time being. The new procedure is explained in Chapter 3 – *The Future for Divorce*.

At the moment to get a divorce in this country you have to prove to the satisfaction of the court that your marriage has broken down irretrievably, in other words that there is no hope for it. There are five possible ways to prove that a marriage has irretrievably broken down.

Adultery

You must prove that your husband or wife has committed adultery, you do not have to name the person with whom your husband or wife has committed adultery. If you wish to do so, that person will then become the 'co-respondent'.

If you are relying on your husband's or wife's adultery in your petition, the court must also be satisfied that you 'find it intolerable to live with' him or her, meaning you can no longer stand the situation of living together.

The odd thing is that you can, in fact, live with your husband or wife for up to six months after the adultery, and still be granted a decree. But if you live together for more than six months after the adultery, you cannot petition for a divorce on the basis of the adultery.

'Living together' means as husband and wife. Obviously, there are situations where people simply have to go on living under the same roof even after the marriage has completely broken down. If they are living separate lives under the same roof, that does not count as 'living together'.

But usually it will be enough for a decree to be granted if your husband or wife admits the adultery.

Unreasonable Behaviour

This is the most 'popular' ground in petitions. You have to prove that your husband or wife has behaved so badly that it is not reasonable that you should be expected to live with him or her.

An obvious example of such behaviour would be where a husband or wife has been physically violent to the other person and has caused injury. But the behaviour need not be as bad as that, although it needs to be reasonably serious.

Even so, behaviour which seems unbearable to one person may be quite acceptable to someone else. One man got a divorce because his wife gave the cats better meals than she gave him. A woman succeeded in persuading a court that her husband was unreasonable because his do-it-yourself efforts around the house were conducted at a snail's pace, leaving her to cope over many months with such inconveniences as a doorless toilet.

Desertion

You would be entitled to a divorce if your husband or wife had walked out on you at least two years ago and had not returned.

Living Apart for Two Years with Consent

If you and your husband or wife have been living apart for at least two years, and you both agree that you want to divorce, you will be entitled to a decree.

Again, 'living apart' can include living separately under the same roof. If you have been sleeping in separate rooms, eating your meals separately, not doing things like laundry or cooking for one another, and not going out socially together, that can count as living apart even though you have been living at the same address.

Living Apart for Five Years

Where a husband and wife have been living apart for at least five years, either of them can apply for a divorce whether or not the other agrees.

What you will Need to Do

You will need to collect three copies of form D8 (divorce petition) from a divorce County Court office or from the Principal Registry of the Family Division in London. If you have children under the age of eighteen you will also need three copies of Form D8A – statement of arrangements for the children. Offices are open from 10 am until 4 pm Monday to Friday, apart from bank holidays. Telephone books have the addresses of County Courts or you can enquire at a Citizen's Advice Bureau or a post office for the address.

One copy of form D8 is for you to keep, one copy is for the court and one copy is for the court to send to your husband or wife. If your petition is on the ground of adultery and you have named the other person (the co-respondent) you will need an extra copy of form D8 for the court to serve on the co-respondent.

If you think you may not have to pay a fee for one of the reasons set out earlier in this chapter you will need a form Ex160 to make your application for a fee exemption or remission. You have to fill in a separate form Ex160 for each fee to be paid. The court will give you some notes to help you fill in the petition, but if you need help with that, or with filling in any of the forms, a Citizen's Advice Bureau (address in the local phone book) can help.

However, people who will help you there are usually not trained lawyers and will not be able to give you legal advice. If you need the help of a solicitor you may be able to get it under what is called the 'Green Form' scheme. Not every firm of solicitors will give this type of advice. Those who are prepared to advise legally aided clients will have the 'Legal Aid' logo displayed somewhere so that you can recognise them.

The Statement of Arrangements

In divorce proceedings, the court will be concerned with any 'child of the family' – this means any child born to you and the respondent, or who has been treated by you as though he or she had been born to you, who is:

(a) under 16 years old; or

(b) between 16 and 18 and still attending school or college full time.

If you have adopted a child, he or she will be a child of your family. However, children placed with you as foster parents are not children of the family.

The court must consider the arrangements you propose to make for the children after the divorce. In exceptional circumstances, your final decree of divorce might be held up until the court considers that the arrangements made for the children are satisfactory.

The Information the Court Needs about the Children

The court will want to know:

(a) where the children live;

(b) who they live with;

(c) whether they will see the other parent and how often;

(d) about their day to day care;

(e) about their health;

(f) where they go to school;

(g) what financial support they will get from the parent with whom they do not live;

(h) if any special arrangements to help or protect them have been made.

The court no longer has to make orders about these matters, and this will be more fully explained in the section on 'Children'. It is much better for your children if you and your husband or wife, as their parents, can make decisions about their future. The law is that the court should never make an order about children unless it is satisfied that making the order would be better for the children than having no order.

Staff at the court will give you a copy of Form D8A (statement of arrangements for children) which you can fill in to explain the arrangements you are making for them. The court will send a copy to your husband or wife asking them to fill in another form (Form 10) to say whether or not they agree with your plans for the children. If there is no agreement, your husband or wife can make their own proposals on a form D8A and send it to the court. The court will send you a copy.

If the court is satisfied with the arrangements set out on your form D8A you will be sent a notice which tells you so.

The judge could decide:

(a) that he or she needs further information about the children – you will be told what this information is; or

(b) that an appointment should be made for both parents to see the judge; or

(c) that a court welfare officer should prepare a report about the children [see Chapter 8]; or

(d) that it would be better for the children if the court made an order.

If the judge decides that the court should make an order about the children, you will need to make a formal application to the court. It will almost always be advisable to consult a solicitor about this. The orders which the court can make are set out in the section on 'Children'.

After the Petition has been Filed

The court will send a copy of the petition to your husband or wife, and to the co-respondent (the person with whom adultery has been committed) if there is one. The respondent (your husband or wife) and the co-respondent, if any, will be given eight days from service (i.e. when you receive it) to let the court know that the petition has been received.

The document which is sent to the court by respondent is called an 'acknowledgement of service' (form D10). The court will send you a copy of this.

If the address you gave the court is incorrect, possibly because the respondent or co-respondent has moved, the post office will return the forms to the court. The court will inform you about this. If you want to carry on with the divorce you will have to find out the correct address and let the court have it. The court will then post the forms to the new address.

What the Respondent Can Do

When your petition is sent by the court, your husband or wife (the respondent) and the co-respondent (if there is one) may react in one of three ways.

Some people simply ignore the petition, or tear it up and put it in the rubbish bin. Others fill in their form D10 and tell the court that they do not agree with your petition and intend to fight it.

The third possibility is what happens most often. Most husbands and wives are not taken by surprise when they receive a petition as they will probably have already discussed the divorce with their partners. Others may just be ready, to agree that the marriage has broken down irretrievably. These people simply fill in the form D10 saying that they agree with the petition, and then return the form to the court.

If form D10 is returned to the court in your case, the court will send you a copy. The Lord Chancellor's Leaflet 4, which can be obtained at the divorce county court, tells you what to do next.

What Happens if the Respondent does not Return the Acknowledgement of Service?

When eight days have passed since the petition was sent and no form D1O has come back, you can ask the court's representative [called the 'court bailiff'] to give a copy of the petition to the respondent personally. You will need to complete another form requesting 'service' by the bailiff. Sometimes the court will automatically send you two copies of this form, but you may have to ask the court for copies yourself.

With them you must send a photograph of the respondent, if possible. If not, you must give a written description of him or her, mentioning the approximate height, the colour of eyes and hair and what sort of build the person is physically. Any other characteristic which might help a stranger to recognise him or her should be mentioned, for example 'walks with a limp'.

You will have to pay a fee for each person to be served, unless you are on income support or receiving family credit.

It will not matter if a co-respondent cannot be found or will not co-operate, but you must be able to show the court that you have taken every reasonable step to trace the respondent and inform him or her about the divorce petition.

What Happens Next

When the court sends copies of the acknowledgement (form D1O) you must check what the respondent or co-respondent has written in answer to the question: 'Do you intend to defend the case?'

If the answer to that question is 'no' you can then ask the court to consider whether you have grounds for a divorce and whether the arrangements that you are suggesting for your children are satisfactory. This is called 'applying for directions for trial'.

If the respondent or co-respondent answers 'yes' you must wait for 29 days from the day they say they received your petition. This is the period during which they must file their defence to the petition which is called an 'answer'.

If, after 29 days, you have not received a copy of an answer, you can then apply for directions for trial. (See under 'Final Procedure below).

If you do receive an answer to your petition, you should ask the advice of a solicitor about how to deal with it.

The Final Procedure

If the respondent returns the acknowledgment of service, and do not want to defend the divorce, the next step is to 'apply for directions for trial'. This involves completing two forms, D84 and D80, which can be obtained free of charge from the court office. There are different kinds of form D80 depending upon which ground you have relied upon in your petition. Make sure you are given the form which matches up to your ground – adultery, behaviour and so on.

When you have filled in both forms you can send or take them to the court office, but not before nine days have passed since the respondent (and any co-respondent) say they, received your petition.

Form D80 is an affidavit, which means that you have to swear that what you have written in it is true in front of someone who is qualified to witness you signing the affidavit. This means that you must not sign D80 until you are in the presence of a solicitor or an officer of the court or Principal Registry.

A solicitor will charge you a fee for witnessing your affidavit. The documents attached ['exhibited'] to your affidavit must show:

(a) that the respondent and the co-respondent [if any] have received a copy of the petition;

(b) if the ground in the petition is adultery, that the respondent and any named co-respondent admit to having committed the adultery;

(c) if the ground is that you have lived apart for two years and the respondent consents to a divorce, the documents must show that he or she has consented;

(d) that the respondent agrees with the arrangements proposed for the children.

In nearly every case, the form D10 (acknowledgment of service) filled in and signed by the respondent will show all of these things. A copy of it should be exhibited (attached) to the affidavit.

Getting the Divorce

All the papers connected with your case will be given to a judge. The judge considers all the papers and decides if you can have a divorce. You do not need to come to court when this is done.

If you have children, the judge will carefully consider the arrangements which you are proposing to make for them and which you have set out in the documents.

If the judge decides to grant you a divorce, the court will send you, your husband or wife, and any co-respondent a certificate saying that you are entitled to a decree. On the certificate will be a time and date for the pronouncement of the decree. There is no need to attend court for this. The name of the case is read out, usually with a list of other cases, and the judge simply says that he pronounces a decree.

You will then be sent a document called a 'decree nisi'. Although this is a divorce decree, it does not mean that you are finally divorced. You are not finally divorced until the decree has been made 'absolute'.

You can normally obtain your decree absolute six weeks after the date of the decree nisi. Sometimes, where there are children of the family, the court will hold up the decree absolute for longer than six weeks, so that matters concerning the children can be considered. If the court is going to do this, you will be informed.

You need yet another form to make your decree absolute and again you can obtain it from the court office. The fee when you apply for decree absolute changes from time to time. Court staff will tell you what it is. If you are on income support, or in receipt of family credit, you may not have to pay anything.

What happens if the Judge Refuses to Give me a Divorce?

Occasionally the court will notify you that the judge has decided that your case is not in order and that a decree of divorce cannot be granted on the information available to the court. If the court needs further information you will be told what information is needed. If the judge feels that your case cannot be decided on the written information which he or she has, there may have to be a court hearing. If there is to be a court hearing, you will have to come to court and give evidence. It would be advisable to consult a solicitor if this happens.

Judicial Separation

It may be that for some reason, religious beliefs for example, you would prefer a judicial separation to a divorce. Judicial separations can be obtained on the same grounds as those for divorce but husbands and wives who have been judicially separated are not free to remarry.

Religious Marriages

Roman Catholics, Jews, Muslims and members of other religions may wish to apply for a religious dissolution of their marriage in addition to a civil divorce. Some useful addresses are given at the end of this chapter.

Defended Divorces

Most divorces are now undefended, which means that the respondent allows the petition to go ahead. This does not mean, of course, that most respondents agree with what is said in the divorce petition. On the contrary, the majority of respondents deeply resent the allegations made against them in the petition, and sincerely believe that they are, at best, wild exaggerations.

The sole ground for divorce in this country is that the marriage has irretrievably broken down. In some countries it is sufficient to establish that both parties agree that the marriage has broken down for a divorce to be granted.

Under the old divorce law, it is not sufficient for the parties simply to agree that their marriage has broken down irretrievably for a divorce to be granted, unless they have been living apart for two years.

As has already been explained, the requirement under the old law is that the irretrievable breakdown of a marriage should be proved in one of five specific ways. These are adultery, unreasonable behaviour, desertion for a period of two years, living apart for two years if both parties agree and living apart for five years.

Perhaps not too surprisingly, it is the unreasonable behaviour petitions which really cause the problems. The formal wording of the petition claims that the respondent has behaved in such a way that it is unreasonable for the petitioner to be expected to live with him or her. It is understandably hurtful to be told that you have behaved so badly that your wife or husband should not be expected to live with you any more.

The natural reaction is to want to retaliate. 'I may have done that, but what about the time she . . .?' or 'Put in those words what I did looks pretty terrible but, let's face it, there was quite a bit of provocation.'

The first reaction for many respondents, when they receive a petition making allegations about their behaviour, is that they want to defend, or even to cross petition, for divorce themselves. But when they ask about this, they will almost invariably be advised that they should allow the petition to proceed undefended. This is very good advice.

Defending a petition can be an extremely costly business. You might, of course, think of defending it in person, without instructing a lawyer. This is possible and a few people actually do it. But what you must bear in mind is that, if you are not successful in defending the petition, even if you avoid paying lawyers to represent you, the court can still make an order for costs against you. This would mean that you would have to pay all the costs of the petitioner, including the cost of lawyers.

A very common anxiety for respondents to petitions based on behaviour is that the allegations made against them, if allowed to go undefended, might count against them when it comes to a dispute about the future of the children of the family, or about finance. However, it is possible to make it clear, when acknowledging service of a petition and indicating no intention to defend, that this is on a 'without prejudice' basis and that you reserve the right to dispute the allegations when other matters are being considered by the court.

Another possibility, if there is one particularly wounding allegation, something about behaviour towards a child of the family for example, is to try to get the petitioner to agree to delete that allegation, on the basis that you will allow the petition to proceed undefended if that allegation is taken out.

It is, of course, always important to remember that even when a petition has been filed, it is still not too late for the marriage to be saved. Skilled counselling can still be tried, if both parties to the marriage are willing to attempt a reconciliation. Sometimes it is only when a respondent actually reads the petition, and sees what is upsetting the petitioner to the point of wanting a divorce, that he or she realises how serious the problems have become. It might not be too late. It is nearly always worth considering whether you really want to part, especially if you have children.

All that having been said, there are still some respondents who do not feel able to allow the petition to go undefended. They want to defend, either on the basis that they have not committed the adultery alleged or that they have not done the other things which the petition alleges amount to unreasonable behaviour.

A respondent can choose simply to defend, to say that the marriage has not broken down irretrievably because the allegations made in the petition are untrue. On the other hand, a respondent can agree that the marriage has broken down irretrievably, but deny that he or she is at fault and say that the breakdown is all the fault of the petitioner. The respondent then makes allegations against the petitioner, of adultery or of unreasonable behaviour. This is called cross petitioning.

Whether the respondent is simply defending, or is defending and cross petitioning, the matter has to go to court and be heard by a judge.

Both husband and wife will have to give evidence before the judge and be cross examined. This can obviously be an extremely distressing experience and will inevitably increase feelings of bitterness and acrimony. If there are children, the parents should think very carefully about the emotional harm likely to be suffered by them as a result.

Useful Addresses

Marriage Care (formerly Catholic Marriage Advisory Council)
Clitherow House
1 Blythe Mews
Blythe Road
London W14 0NW
Telephone: 0171 371 1341

Jewish Marriage Council
23 Ravenshurst Avenue
London NW4 4EE
Telephone: 0181 203 6311
Crisis Helpline: 01345 581999

The Family Welfare Association
501-505 Kingsland Road
London E8 4AU
Telephone: 0171 254 6251

One Plus One
14 Theobalds Road
London WC1X 8PF
Telephone: 0171 831 5261

Solicitors Family Law Association [SFLA]
PO Box 302
Keston
Kent BR2 6EZ
Telephone: 01689 850227

Your local Citizen's Advice Bureau can also help – address and telephone number in local telephone directory.

If you are already divorced, separated or widowed, support and advice is available from:

The Beginning Experience
1 Apple Tree Walk
Clymping
Near Littlehampton
West Sussex BN17 5QN
Telephone: 01903 722230

African Caribbean Family Mediation Service
Mediation on Children Issues
2–4 St John's Crescent
Brixton
London SW9 7LX
Telephone: 0171 737 2366

Family Mediation Service
Mediation on Children Issues
267 Ballards Lane
Finchley
London N12 8NR
Telephone: 0181 343 9899

Divorce Mediation and Counselling Service
38 Ebury Street
London SW1W 0LU
Telephone: 0171 730 2422

Eye to Eye Mediation
231 Camberwell New Road
London SE5 0TH
Telephone: 0171 701 1114/703 2532

Mediation for Families (East London and City)
74 Great Eastern Street
London EC2A 3JL
Telephone: 0171 613 1666

The Family Mediation Service – Institute of Family Therapy
24-32 Stephenson Way
London NW1 2HX
Telephone: 0171 391 9150

South-East London Family Mediation Bureau
5 Upper Park Road
Bromley
Kent BR1 3HN
Telephone: 0181 460 4606

A book that could be helpful is
Breaking Up without Cracking Up
by Christopher Compson (Harper Collins £6.99).

CHAPTER TWO

WHO GETS WHAT
WHEN YOU SPLIT UP?

Questions about money and property tend to come up in almost every relationship breakdown. In some cases, of course, there is no difficulty. If two people have been married or living together, there is no property, they have no children, and each of them has a job, there should be no problems about finances or property when their relationship founders. But in most relationships the financial facts are not quite so straightforward. For example, when only one partner has been in employment, with the other staying at home to care for their children throughout the relationship, or when they have been purchasing a house or flat on a mortgage, someone has to decide who gets what when they separate. It is a hard but inescapable fact of life that two households are not going to be able to live as cheaply as one did.

Even where two people have been living in rented accommodation, particularly if rented from the local authority, this can be an important asset and complications can arise.

If your relationship is breaking down, and you have decided to separate, the first step is to see whether you can agree between you what is to happen about finance and about any property which you may own. If you can't agree, you should definitely attempt to get some mediator or conciliator to help you. Why? One good reason is that to reach agreement with the help of mediation will be much cheaper than asking the court to decide what should happen. Even if you are legally aided, you may still have to meet the costs of lawyers and a court hearing yourself in the end. But if you can't even reach agreement with the help of mediation, the law is the last resort.

Married Couples

It used to be the case that if a married woman owned any property or earned any money, it belonged to her husband. It is less than 150 years since the law began to give a wife some rights over her own finances. The courts can now make orders that one partner in a marriage – usually the husband, but it can be the wife – should make regular payments for the maintenance of the other. The courts can also make orders for dividing between the husband and wife any capital assets, such as houses, flats, savings, or pension entitlements.

Even if you have not actually filed a divorce petition, you can still obtain an order for maintenance in a court if your husband (or wife) should support you and is refusing to do so.

Since the child support law came into force in 1993, things have changed completely so far as the maintenance of children is concerned. The decision about how much maintenance should be paid for a child, and making sure the parent pays that amount, are now under the control of a government agency, the Child Support Agency. The courts no longer come into the picture so far as maintenance of children is concerned, unless there are very exceptional circumstances. 'Child Support' is discussed fully in Chapter 9.

What are your Rights to Money and Property if your Marriage ends?

When a marriage has broken down, the law has given the court power to make any orders about finances or property which seem to the court to be just. The power of the court includes the power to order that maintenance payments should be made by one ex-partner to the other. The court can also make orders which affect property or other capital assets which one or both of the partners to the marriage may own. In most cases, of course, the most important asset which a couple have is the home in which they have lived together.

That home may be in the sole name of the husband. He alone may have provided the deposit when it was purchased, and he may have paid off the instalments on the mortgage entirely from his own earnings. He might have other capital assets, savings in a building society for example, a boat or an expensive car. He might own his own business and have a great deal of capital invested in that. He may have a substantial entitlement to a pension to which he has contributed over many years.

Less often, the wife may be wealthy in her own right. She may own property, or valuable jewellery, for example. She could be a successful businesswoman or a professional woman with capital assets, substantial savings or pension entitlement.

The court will look at every bit of property or capital owned by the husband and by the wife. It then looks at the facts of the particular marriage to help it decide what orders it can make which will be fair to everyone. When it does so, it has to keep in mind that, if there are any children of the marriage, the interests of the children will be the most important consideration. This means, for example, that the parent who has the children living with him or her will be more likely to keep the home, at least until the children have all reached the age of seventeen, or finish full time education.

What does the Court take into Account?

When a court has to make decisions about money or property (ancillary matters as they are called), there are certain things which have to be taken into account by law. If a judge should make an order about money or property which does not properly consider all these matters, the order would be appealable.

1. Resources

The first thing which a judge must do, when he is deciding how money or property ought to be divided after a divorce, is to look at the resources of the husband and the wife. The resources will include the income of each, the earning capacity which each has and any property which each of them owns. It is important to remember that, when the court is considering earning capacity, it does not simply look at what each partner is earning at the time when the matter comes before the court. Often, the wife will not have been earning money for some years because she has been looking after young children. If the children have all started at school, for example, the judge might decide that the mother has skills which give her an earning capacity, even if it is only to be on a part-time basis. If the mother happened to have some qualification, in teaching or nursing perhaps, that would be taken into account. Or it might be possible for the mother to undergo some training to improve skills which she already has, such as computer skills, in order to get her into the job market again.

However, the court will always look at all the facts. A mother who has not been in employment for twenty years will not be expected to go straight out and earn her own living. The ages of her children will be an important consideration, and the state of the job market in her locality will also be taken into account.

The court will also consider resources which either the husband or the wife are likely to have in the foreseeable future. Two such examples are illustrated in the following case studies.

CASE STUDY

Marjorie and Kenneth are divorcing, having been married for nine years. They have two young children, who will be living with Marjorie. They have always lived in rented accommodation and neither of them has any substantial capital or savings. Kenneth's wealthy aunt died shortly after he and Marjorie separated. Under the terms of his aunt's will Kenneth has been left £100,000, which he will receive in the near future. Can Marjorie expect to be awarded some of that money by the court?

The answer is that in all those circumstances it is likely that Marjorie would be given a lump sum by the court to be paid by Kenneth from his expected inheritance. That £100,000 is a resource which he is likely, indeed certain, to have in the foreseeable future and it can consequently be brought into consideration by the court.

On the other hand, had Kenneth's wealthy aunt been a woman still in her fifties and in excellent health, it is unlikely that the court would take Kenneth's prospects of an inheritance from her into account. She might not leave him anything at all in her will and she might well live for another 30 years or more.

CASE STUDY

Julie and Tim are divorcing after nine years of marriage. They have no children. Tim has always been the breadwinner while Julie stayed at home as a housewife throughout he marriage. Julie is asking the court to order that Tim should pay maintenance for her. Since their separation, a few months ago, Julie has been doing a course in bookkeeping. She is doing well on the course and expects to qualify as a bookkeeper in six months' time. The court will take into account the fact that Julie can reasonably be expected to get her bookkeeping qualifications and then to find a job so that she can support herself. If the court is satisfied that bookkeeping jobs will be available within a reasonable distance of where Julie is living, the order for Tim to pay her maintenance may well take account of the situation by providing for the payments to be made only for a certain length of time, say twelve months, to give Julie a chance to get on her feet and be self-supporting.

Every case is unique, of course, and there are many other important considerations for the court, so that Marjorie, Kenneth, Julie and Tim can only be examples of what might happen.

2. Needs, Obligations and Responsibilities

Once the court has determined the resources of a husband and wife, the needs, obligations and responsibilities of each have to be taken into account. The most obvious need for anyone is some sort of roof over his or her head. The court will do its utmost to try to ensure that both husband and wife have a home at the end of the day.

Desirable as it is for each of the divorcing partners to have a home, this cannot always be achieved. If there are children of the family, the court will always give priority to providing a home for them. This means that the parent with whom the children are to live will almost always be the one who will be allowed to remain in the former matrimonial home where there is not enough money to provide two homes.

Because the mother is often, although not by any means always, the parent with whom the children will live, it is often the mother who stays in the matrimonial home. This has given rise to a view, fairly common among fathers, that the courts favour mothers when it comes to financial matters in divorce proceedings.

The courts try to be as fair as possible, while remaining mindful that the needs of the children have to come first. In many cases the mother will be allowed to stay in the home with the children, but

34   *Law and the Family*

only until the children are of school leaving age. At that stage, the court may say that the home should be sold and the net proceeds divided between the husband and wife in whatever proportions the court considers just.

It cannot be said too often that every case has its own individual set of facts. This means that it is impossible to be certain about what might or might not happen in any particular case. There are so many factors to be taken into account that the best that can be attempted is an 'educated guess'.

3. Contributions

The court will take into account the contributions to the marriage made by the husband and the wife. The husband may have made all the financial contributions and might think that, because of that, the wife should not be entitled to claim anything.

But in many marriages where the husband has been the sole earner and contributor of money, the wife has played her part by bringing up the children, cleaning, washing, ironing and cooking for all the family, and generally carrying out all the work lumped together as 'being a housewife'.

The courts take the view that the sort of contribution made by a wife who stays at home to care for the home, the husband and their children is equally as important as that of the man who goes out and earns the money.

4. Age

The ages of the husband and wife can affect the decision of the court about financial matters.

CASE STUDY

Doreen, a 55 year old wife, has stayed at home caring for her family for 30 years. In that time her husband Frank, who is the same age, has built up his own reasonably profitable business, from the proceeds of which he has supported Doreen and their family. It will be difficult, if not impossible, for Frank to persuade the court that Doreen ought to go out and get a job and be self-supporting to relieve him of the liability to maintain her in the future.

It has been said by the courts that 'marriage is not a

meal ticket for life'. Although this reflects the court's hope
that partners to a broken marriage can eventually become
financially independent of one another, judges are realists.
Women of 55, with no special qualifications or skills and
who have been out of the job market for 30 years, are not
likely to be able to find jobs in today's conditions.

   Doreen has made her contribution to the marriage over
the years. Unless Frank is in a financial position to pay her a
large sum of money to compensate her for loss of maintenance in the future, his liability to maintain her would be
likely to continue.

The length of the marriage is important too.

CASE STUDY

Ben is a millionaire. He meets Audrey, who has no money at
all. They marry, but very quickly realise that the marriage is
a mistake and separate after only a year. There are no children. Can Audrey expect substantial financial provision from
Ben?

   The answer will almost certainly be "no" although she
might get an order for a limited period if she needs time to
find a job.

5. Is Behaviour Taken into Account?

People are in a very vulnerable state at the time of the breakdown of
their relationship. Often, extremely hurtful things are said and done,
because when you are hurt yourself you usually feel like giving as
good as you get. The husband, the wife, or even both, may behave in
quite outrageous ways. When money and property cases come before the court, it is sometimes difficult for people to resist the temptation to tell the court all about the rotten behaviour of the other
person. Husbands or wives often seem to believe that if their partner
has behaved badly, that ought to affect the amount of money to be
awarded by the court.

   But the court is only allowed to take conduct into account in a
very limited way. The behaviour must be so bad that reasonable person would say that it would be unjust for the court to ignore it. This
standard is a high one, and it means that only in it very few cases will
the behaviour of one of the partners be taken into account when it
comes to deciding on a division of money or property.

In one case, the wife had actually assisted the husband's attempts at suicide, because she was hoping that she would benefit financially on his death. At the same time she had been committing adultery. That behaviour was found by the court to satisfy the test, and the wife's entitlement to financial provision was reduced because of it.

But in another case, where a wife had been committing adultery with a boy half her age who was a guest in the matrimonial home, the judge decided that the wife's behaviour was not bad enough for him to take it into account when deciding financial matters.

6. All the Circumstances

The matters listed above are just some of the important things which the court must take into account when deciding financial and property cases in divorce, but they are by no means the only things which will be considered. The law requires that the judge take into account all the circumstances in any particular case and, as every case is unique it means that advising on financial matters in divorce is not at all an easy task.

Also remember that judges are human beings, with their own, very often unconscious, prejudices and opinions. The vast majority of them are skilled professionals and are dedicated to being as fair as they can be to both parties in any case which comes before them. That does not mean, however, that there is only one obvious outcome to every case.

Reaching an Agreement without Going to Court

It is quite impossible for anyone to be absolutely certain of what the court will decide in any particular case. It is therefore extremely important for you to think very carefully about whether you can possibly come to an agreement about your money and property when you divorce. This avoids the uncertainty, the delay – and the considerable expense! – of a court hearing.

Agreements have another advantage. It is unlikely that either the husband or the wife will get exactly what he or she has been hoping for, as a result of the agreement. But at least, even if each has been a little disappointed, at the same time a compromise has been reached which each is prepared to accept.

Once you go though the door of the court you are completely at the mercy of what the judge will decide. That might be a decision which is utterly devastating in its effect, on one side or the other. It can be, and surprisingly often is, a decision about which neither party feels particularly happy.

If you do decide to reach an agreement without the court, assistance with negotiating settlements in financial matters is available' through mediation organisations. Professionally trained mediators, who are strictly neutral in their approach, are available to help and advise on what would be a fair settlement in any case. The fees charged involve couples in much less expense than the costs of a court battle. The process is far less of a strain on the emotions than an appearance in court, which most people find a huge ordeal.

If you do reach agreement, the agreement can be made into a court order by consent, without the necessity of anyone actually going to the court to give evidence.

Some Orders which the Court can Make

In divorce proceedings there are several types of order which the court can make. The most common orders are given below.

1. Maintenance Orders

Orders can be made that one spouse makes maintenance, or periodical payments, to the other (usually the husband to the wife). The payments are normally made on a weekly or monthly basis. They can be ordered for a set period. For example, in the case where Julie was training to be a bookkeeper (page 32) the court might order Tim to make periodical payments to her for a period of only twelve months.

It is the hope and the aim of the courts that husbands and wives will eventually become financially independent of one another, so that the 'meal ticket for life' situation does not arise. But in the case of Doreen and Frank (page 34), we saw that it is not always possible for the court to take the view that someone is capable of achieving financial independence.

If a husband fails to make payments under a court order, enforcement proceedings can be taken in the court where the order was made. If the husband is in employment it is possible to obtain an attachment of earnings order to ensure that his employers deduct the amount he should be paying from his wages and then pay it to the wife directly.

If, for some reason, it is not possible to obtain an attachment of earnings order, a husband who persistently fails to comply with a court order for maintenance could eventually be sent to prison.

Maintenance orders can be varied if there is a change in circumstances. If the husband loses his job he can apply, to vary, the payments downwards. If the wife, for example, has a part-time job and loses that she can apply for a variation to increase the maintenance order. You will find more information on maintenance, in particular on child support legislation, in Chapter 9.

2. Lump Sum Orders

The court can order a husband or a wife to make a payment of a lump sum of money to the other party. This sum can be of any amount, depending upon the assets of the parties in any particular case. This can be ordered in addition to maintenance payments, or it can be a final settlement of the financial obligations of the payer.

3. Transfers of Property

The court can order a husband or a wife to transfer any property which belongs to that person to the other spouse. This order is most often made when the property to be transferred is the former matrimonial home of the parties. In the particular circumstances of a case, it may be decided by the court that, for example, the wife should have the husband's share of a jointly owned home transferred to her.

Property includes tenancies, which can be very a valuable asset, and other forms of property, company shares, for example.

Pensions and Divorce

In dealing with financial aspects of divorce in the past, little, if any, attention may have been given to any pension entitlement which one partner (usually the husband) might have, particularly in cases where some years would have to pass before such a pension became payable. It has now been recognised that in many marriages the husband's pension entitlement can be one of the most important capital assets, sometimes worth even more than the matrimonial home.

As has already been said, it has been recognised for over 30 years that the contribution which is made by a wife (as mother and home-maker) is to be taken into account just as that made by a husband, who has been the sole breadwinner for the family. By making that contribution, such a wife will have, indirectly, contributed towards the pension expectations of her husband. The courts had already begun to take pension entitlement into consideration but the law now gives more power to judges to ensure that wives are fairly treated when it comes to these assets.

The power is called 'earmarking' and means that a judge can decide that, when a man (or woman) becomes entitled to a lump sum and/or annuity benefit under a pension scheme, the court can ear-mark a proportion of either or both for his or her partner. The law in earmarking pensions has only come into force in recent years. It does not mean that anyone will automatically be given an interest in a spouse's pension, however, it does mean that the question of pension entitlement should always be a factor taken into consideration by the courts when it comes to looking at all the circumstances of the financial situation.

The Powers of the Court

From all this you can see that when a marriage breaks down, the courts have almost limitless power and discretion to look at the whole picture: the needs of the husband and wife, the overriding necessity to put the welfare of any children of the family first, the assets available by way of income and capital and the contributions made by each of the parties to the marriage.

Taking these, and all the other considerations mentioned, into account, the court does the best it can to ensure that the assets of the parties are as fairly divided up between them as possible, bearing in mind of course the overriding concern for any children.

These powers of the court when marriages break down are not, however, available when a non-married relationship breaks down.

Unmarried Couples

Marriage has rather gone out of fashion. In the days of our grandparents, if a man and woman had decided to live openly together in a sexual relationship without getting married they would have had a hard time of it, particularly the woman. Even in our own parents' time, a couple in that position would have been unusual and would have caused a lot of gossip. But there was quite a bit of hypocrisy in those days too. If a couple had been careful to avoid making their relationship so obvious that it could not be ignored, other people might be prepared to turn a blind eye.

There was also, of course, the double standard. Men were allowed to behave in ways for which women would be condemned. The ultimate disgrace was for an unmarried woman to have a baby. Not only would she suffer the consequences for the rest of her life, her unfortunate and blameless child would be branded for life as well.

The situation is very different today. Large numbers of young couples are choosing to live together without going through a ceremony of marriage. There are many reasons for this. Undoubtedly, one of the main reasons is that fewer people now have any strong religious beliefs. Also the fact that so many marriages break down today has definitely contributed to the increase in the numbers of couples who choose to live together without marriage.

Many young couples think that they should try living together for a few years, just to see how it works out, rather than marry straight away. The snag about this is that it seems that marriages between partners who have already been living together for some years are no more likely to survive than those where the partners do not start living together until after the marriage ceremony has taken place.

The sheer expense of getting married puts a lot of people off. In May 1998, *Wedding & Home* magazine calculated the cost of an average wedding to be £10,151, a great deal more money than most young couples, or their parents, could run to. One enterprising vicar was convinced that the question of cost was at the root of the reluctance of local couples to marry in his church. So he paid for advertising space in local newspapers and on local radio and television programmes. In the media he announced that his church was offering a cut-price package deal for marriages. The deal would include fees for the use of the church and the organist, flowers, lighting and caretaking. The bargain package would cost less than a third of what the cost of all this would normally amount to. He really boosted the number of requests for weddings at his church!

Does the Law Recognise Common Law Marriage?

You often hear people talk about something which they call 'common law marriage', when a couple have lived as husband and wife for a certain length of time, just as if they had been married. In this situation shouldn't they have exactly the same rights as though they had been through a ceremony of marriage?

Unfortunately for a large number of disillusioned people – usually women – the answer is no. The law does not recognise any such thing as common law marriage. As far as the law is concerned you are either married or you are not, and it does not matter for how long you may have lived as husband and wife, nor does it matter whether everyone you know believed that you were married.

Sometimes even the children of a family believe that their parents are married when in fact they are not. This might not matter very much in some cases but it can have very sad results in others.

CASE STUDY

When Noel died, he left his 'wife' Siobhan and their teenage children in the home which he had owned in his sole name. A few months after Noel's death, Carmel appeared on the doorstep and informed the family that she had been Noel's wife before he had formed his relationship with Siobhan. They had never been divorced and Noel and Siobhan had lived together without getting married. Carmel produced a will in which Noel had left everything to her. He had never made another will. Had he been divorced and later married Siobhan, his marriage would have revoked the old will. But in the circumstances, Carmel was entitled to the home occupied by Siobhan and her children.

When you come to think about it, it would be almost impossible to find a fair test which would establish something like a common law marriage. How long would the couple have to live together for common law marriage to be recognised? Would it have to be a longer period if the couple had not had children together? What would happen if one, or both, had already legally married someone else?

It is difficulties like these that make it unlikely that such 'common law' marriages will ever be granted the set of legal rights which comes with marriage. So far as children are concerned, that really does not matter very much today. A non-married parent can have exactly the same responsibilities and rights as a married parent. There is more about this in the chapter on parental responsibility in the 'Children' section of this book. But so far as property rights are concerned, whether you have been married or not makes all the difference to what you can expect to get if your relationship breaks down.

When two people decide to live together as man and wife without going through a ceremony of marriage, the commitment they make to one another is usually one of love. At such an exciting and romantic time the last thing they want to do is plan what will happen if they split up.

They may have chosen not to get married because they don't believe in marriage or they are disillusioned with the whole idea of matrimony. Or perhaps they feel that they want to wait for a time, to save up to have a lovely wedding day when they can afford it. Or maybe one would really have liked to get married while the other does not feel quite so committed. They may tell each other that it would be better to wait a few years, to see how things work out. Or one or both may already be married to someone else. For any of these reasons, or maybe for some other reason, they just move in together, without getting married, and set up home. No need for meaningless bits of paper, they may think. We know we love one another and that is enough.

But is it? When a relationship like that does last, it may be quite indistinguishable from a loving partnership between two people who have taken vows together in church, chapel, synagogue, temple or register office, and who have a marriage certificate to prove it.

It is when the relationship founders that the difference so often becomes all too stark, because the law does not give the protection to unmarried partners that it provides for those who are married. All too often, in a situation where an unmarried relationship breaks down, it is the woman who gets the raw end of the deal.

CASE STUDY

When Tina met Rod they were instantly attracted to one

another. They enjoyed the same music, liked one another's friends, shared the same sense of humour. After a few months they realised that they were in love and wanted to live together. Tina was sharing a rented flat with two other girls. Rod was buying his flat on a mortgage. When they decided to live together, the obvious thing to do was for Tina to move into Rod's flat, which she did. They were short of money, so although marriage was discussed they decided to wait for a time to see how things worked out and when they could afford a wedding. As time passed, the subject of getting married just never seemed to come up again.

Both Tina and Rod had well-paid jobs in the computer business. Their earnings were pretty much on a par with each other. It had been agreed that Rod would continue to pay the mortgage and the other outgoings on the flat, including water rates and the bills for gas, electricity and the telephone. Tina would pay for their food, their clothes and their holidays.

Sadly, their relationship did not last. They lived together for ten years. But there came a time when Tina realised that Rod was having an affair with a girl he had met at work. There was a blazing row between them. Tina packed her belongings and left the flat immediately afterwards.

The flat had never been transferred into their joint names. It had simply never occurred to Tina to suggest to Rod that it should be. It was their home and, if she had thought about it at all, she assumed that, by her contributions over the years in paying for the food, the clothes, and the holidays, she would have acquired a fair share in the property. She suggested to Rod that he could raise an extra mortgage to buy out her interest in the flat. Then she could use the money as a deposit on a flat for herself. She knew that Rod would have no difficulty in raising the amount she thought she would be entitled to, on his salary.

But the breakdown of the relationship had been acrimonious. Rod was not in the mood to agree to anything which Tina suggested. 'It's my flat', he told her. 'It's always been my flat. You have no interest in it. You're not entitled to a penny from me.'

Tina was outraged. She went to see a solicitor. She told the solicitor her story and asked how much the solicitor thought her interest in Rod's flat would be worth. Unfortunately for Tina, the answer had to be that Rod was right.

The law is very clear on property rights when people have not been married. Tina had made no actual payments in money towards the mortgage instalments or towards improvements made to the flat, and therefore she had acquired no interest whatsoever in it. 'But what about our agreement – that I would pay for food and holidays and he would pay the other outgoings?' she asked. 'Surely that gives me an interest?'

The solicitor asked if there had been an agreement between her and Rod that she should have an interest in the flat if she paid for their food, clothing and holidays. But there had never been any discussion between Tina and Rod about the ownership of the flat. So, sadly for Tina – and for thousands of women, and some men, who have found themselves in her position – the law could not help.

CASE STUDY

Flo was another unlucky lady. She met George when she was only eighteen years old. George was a widower with three very young children. Flo fell in love with George and moved in to live with him in the house which he was buying on a mortgage. As the eldest child was only six years old, there was no question of Flo going out to work. But she loved children and gladly set about caring for George's home and family, while he went out to work.

Flo brought up George's children but he and she never married. They had been living together for over twenty years when George told her that there was someone else. He told Flo that she would have to leave, as he intended to invite his new girlfriend to live with him.

Flo was devastated. Now in her early forties, she had never had a job outside he home. She had no experience of anything other than being a wife and mother. She, like Tina, had never worried about whether she had an interest in the house which had been her home. She had not expected that her relationship with George would ever come to an end. It was just like a marriage.

When Flo went to see a solicitor, she was given the same bad news. Her contribution as unpaid housekeeper and mother to someone else's children had not given her any right to any interest in the property which had always been in George's sole name, and which he had purchased before they had met. She had never contributed any money towards the purchase of the home. George had never promised her that she would have an interest in it. They had not been married. So she could not claim that she had acquired any right to a share in it.

Had either Tina been married to Rod, or Flo to George, their situation would have been entirely different. On divorce, the courts have huge powers to make orders about what should happen to property. It would not have mattered in the slightest that Rod's flat was in his sole name or George's house in his. Tina's contributions by paying for food, clothes and holidays would have been taken into consideration, even though she had not made any direct contribution towards the mortgage or improvements to the flat. Flo's contribution in caring for the home and the children would have been recognised, even though she had never been able to contribute financially.

Tina and Flo should serve as awful warnings to anyone thinking of setting up home with someone who is already purchasing a property in his or her sole name. It may be less than romantic, but couples who do not marry should sit down and have a full discussion about what is to happen to any property which is to be their home and which one of them is buying on a mortgage, or already owns.

Ideally, if you are both going to contribute in the way in which married couples usually do – either by pooling your earnings or by one bringing up the children while the other has the job – the property should be legally conveyed into your joint names. The conveyance should set out what your respective interests are to be – whether you are going to share equally or, if not, in what proportions the shares are to be. It really, cannot be said often enough that if you are considering living together without getting married you should consult a solicitor if the purchase of any property is involved.

When you Buy Together

Rod and George were already purchasing their homes when they met the women who moved in with them. But many other young couples who live together without marriage actually decide to purchase a property together in their joint names. So is there any problem with that?

The answer is that, again, it must be kept in mind that cohabitation is not marriage. The law cannot do for unmarried couples what it can do for those who have been legally married. It is absolutely essential, if you are thinking about purchasing a property with your partner and you are not married, that you should talk about what interest each of you is to have in the property you are going to buy. This is because so many joint purchasers have been shocked to discover, when their relationship broke down, that the fact that the property is registered in joint names does not mean that they have automatically acquired equal shares in it.

This is an extremely tricky area of law, even for lawyers. Again, it is of the utmost importance to make sure that you consult your solicitor when you decide to buy a home in your joint names. Make it clear to the solicitor what you have decided your respective interests in the property are to be if your relationship breaks down. This might depend on which of you has paid the deposit or on whether one of you has already been buying the property in his or her sole name.

When you are starting out together in a loving relationship, it probably seems incredible to you that someone you love so much could ever behave unfairly or let you down. Unfortunately, the stark reality is that people are being treated shabbily by ex-lovers every day of the week. Try to make sure that it never happens to you or to someone you care about. Remember, if you are going to live together without getting married, you need to protect yourself by thinking ahead to what might happen if it all goes terribly wrong.

CHAPTER THREE

THE FUTURE FOR DIVORCE

In the Family Law Act of 1996, parliament made radical changes to the law relating to divorce. The thinking behind these changes was that the bitterness and acrimony which so often accompany the divorce process might be avoided if the five 'grounds' on which petitions had been based could be abandoned. When the new law comes into force it will not be necessary for the petitioner to make allegations of adultery, unreasonable behaviour or desertion against the respondent, as it is at present.

At the very beginning of the Act, the court, and any person 'exercising functions' under its provisions, is put under an obligation to take into account the following general principles:

(a) that the institution of marriage is to be supported;

(b) that the husband and wife must be encouraged to take all practicable steps, whether by marriage counselling or otherwise, to save the marriage;

(c) that a marriage which has irretrievably broken down and is being brought to an end should be brought to an end –
  (i) with minimum distress to the parties and to the children affected;
  (ii) with the divorce and any questions about the marriage dealt with in a way that means that the husband, the wife and the children will continue to have a good relationship;
  (iii)without unreasonably legal costs;

(d) that any risk of violence to the husband, wife or children be removed or diminished as far as possible.

Divorce and Separation Under the New Law

The court will have power to make two orders:

(a) a divorce order which brings the marriage to an end;

(b) a separation order.

A separation order means just that – it brings the marriage to an end. However, the order will continue to be effective:

(a) for as long as the marriage continues; *or*

(b) until the court cancels it; this must be on the joint application of the parties.

A wife or husband will be able to start proceedings by making a statement that she or he believes that the marriage has broken down. Spouses may also make a joint statement that each of them believes the marriage to have broken down. This statement is to be known as 'the statement of marital breakdown'.

The Information Meeting

Usually, the husband or wife making the statement will have had to attend an information meeting not less than three months before the date when the statement is made. When the husband and wife have decided to make a joint statement, they may attend separate information meetings, or go together to the same meeting.

If only one partner has made the statement saying the marriage has broken down, the other will normally have to attend an information meeting before making any application to the court about a child of the family, or certain property or financial matters, or before opposing the divorce or any application made by the husband and wife who has made the statement.

An information meeting will be conducted by an independent person who:

(a) is properly qualified and specially appointed;

(b) will have no financial or other interest in any marital proceedings between the parties.

The purpose of the information meeting is so that both the husband and wife can get information about the divorce and separation process. It will also provide an opportunity for the husband and wife to meet a marriage guidance counsellor.

More regulations will be made about, among other things,

(a) places and times at which information meetings are to be held;

(b) written information to be given to persons attending them;

(c) giving information to people who, for some reason, are not expected to attend such meetings.

What Sort of Information will be given at the Meetings?

The meetings will provide information about:

(a) marriage counselling and other marriage support services;

(b) the importance of the welfare, wishes and feelings of children;

(c) how parents may be helped to understand the ways in which children can be helped to cope with the breakdown of a marriage;

(d) financial questions which may arise on divorce or separation, and which are available to help the parties;

(e) protection available against violence and how to obtain support and assistance;

(f) mediation;

(g) the availability to each of the parties of independent legal advice and representation;

(h) legal aid and how to get it;

(i) the divorce and separation process.

Reflection and Consideration

If, having attended an information meeting, a wife or husband makes a statement that she or he believes the marriage has broken down, or if they make a joint statement that each believes it has broken down, the next step in the process will be what is called a period for 'reflection and consideration'. This period will be used:

(a) for the parties to reflect on whether the marriage can be saved, and to have a chance to have a reconciliation;

(b) to think about what arrangements should be made for the future.

The period for reflection and consideration will normally be nine months from the fourteenth day after the statement of marriage breakdown is received by the court. As with the present law, it will not be possible to get a divorce or separation by making a statement within a year of the date of the marriage.

If the parties, at any time during the period for reflection and consideration, give notice to the court that they are attempting a reconciliation but require additional time, the period will:

(a) stop running on the day on which the notice is received by the court; but

(b) resume running on the day on which either party gives notice to the court that the attempted reconciliation has been unsuccessful.

(c) if the attempted reconciliation interrupts the period by a continuous eighteen months, a fresh statement will have to be made.

In certain circumstances, the court will be able to extend the period for reflection and consideration.

Arrangements for the Future

Before a divorce or separation order can be made, one of the following will have to be produced to the court:

(a) a court order dealing with the finances;

(b) a negotiated agreement dealing with the finances;

(c) a declaration by both parties that they have made their financial arrangements;

(d) a declaration by one of the parties (to which the other has made no objection) that:
   (i) he or she has no significant assets and does not intend to

make an application for financial provision; and

(ii) he or she believes that the other party has no significant assets and does not intend to make any application for financial provision; and

(iii) there are, therefore, no financial arrangements to be made.

The court will only be able to make a divorce or separation order if it
is satisfied that the requirements about attendance at information
meetings and the arrangements for the future are satisfied.

Orders Preventing Divorce

There will be some circumstances in which the court may make an
order preventing divorce. That sort of order will only be made if the
court is satisfied:

(a) that to dissolve the marriage would result in substantial financial, or other hardship, to the other party, or to a child of the
family; and

(b) that it would be wrong, in all the circumstances (including the
conduct of the parties and the interests of any child of the family)
for the marriage to be dissolved.

It will be very interesting indeed to see whether the courts will in
fact make orders preventing divorce. Rather similar provisions already exist, but case law shows that people have rarely if ever managed to convince the court that a divorce should be refused.

On the past record, it is to be expected that it will be difficult, if
not impossible, to persuade the court of 'substantial financial hardship'.

When will the New Divorce Law Come In?

Pilot scheme information meetings are being tried out in different
areas of the country at the moment. The objective is to test out how
these are working before attendance at them becomes a requirement

throughout the country, possibly in the hope of avoiding the sort of disasters that followed the introduction of the Child Support Agency.

The new law will not be brought into force until these pilot information sessions have been completed and evaluated. At the moment, there is little information available on how they are going, except that it is anticipated that the earliest possible date for the new procedures to replace the old is likely to be some time in the year 2000.

SECTION II

Children

CHAPTER FOUR

HOW THE LAW HAS CHANGED

In an ideal world, the two most important people in the life of any child should be his or her mother and father. Unfortunately, today more and more children are being brought up by one parent alone, by a parent and a step-parent, or even without either of their parents, in the care of a local authority.

The annual divorce rate in the United Kingdom is currently 150,000. In over half of divorcing families, there are children under the age of sixteen. It is estimated that by the year 2000 that 3.7 million children will have experienced parental divorce. Perhaps the saddest statistic of all is that half of these children will have lost all contact with the non-resident parent within three years of the divorce.

Moreover, the figures above take no account of the 33 per cent of children born outside marriage each year whose parents also separate. Nowadays, it is not at all unusual for children to suffer the breakdown of carers' relationships on more than one occasion during their childhood and adolescence.

The law has had to become involved more often with children, partly as a result of the changing patterns in family life, and also because of the numbers of children who have been suffering from the most appalling cruelty through neglect or emotional or physical abuse of some sort. It is becoming impossible to open a newspaper without reading details of yet another case where a child has suffered at the hands of the adults who should be giving that child protection and love.

Why did the Law have to Change?

Until 1989, when the Children Act was passed, the law concerning children was in a complete shambles. In public law, cases about the same child could be brought to court in many different ways. It could, and did, happen that there were cases going on about the same child in two or three different courts during the same period of time. It was a frequent complaint that children were being seriously emotionally damaged by a delay in cases. To a small child a few months can seem an eternity.The younger the child, the more irreversible the damage which could be done by delay.

We are all aware of the tragic cases where small children suffer the most terrible injuries at the hands of violent parents or step-parents, sometimes even resulting in death. Cases like these underlined the need to tighten up the system for protecting children, and for stepping in quickly where there is a real suspicion that a child might be being abused in some way.

Children of Divorce

Divorce was another area where children could be unnecessarily hurt. It is devastating enough for a child when his or her parents decide they no longer love one another, but the rules laid down in divorce cases meant that there could be additional tensions imposed on the family. For example, even in a case where the parents had come to a sensible agreement between themselves about with which parent the children should live, and about how often they should have contact with the other parent, the court still had to make an order. It was almost as though the law took the view that, if your marriage had broken down, you could not be trusted to make decisions about your own children.

If the parents could not agree, they had to battle in court over who should have custody of the children and how much access the other parent should have. Custody came to be looked on almost as ownership of a child. No matter how hard the courts tried to make it clear that even if one parent had legal custody the other was still just as much of a parent, the message was definitely not getting through. Warring parents refused to look on a custody order as anything but a matter of winning or losing. All too often, the parent who got the custody order would then behave as though it meant that the other parent could be excluded from the child's life as far as possible. Every request for access would mean a further skirmish in the battle, in many cases another fight in court. And once again the real casualties would be the children.

Within living memory children were very much the property of their parents. The parents might be good, caring and loving or bad, neglectful and abusive of their children. It was only in the most extreme cases of cruelty that the law would interfere with the way in which children were treated by their carers. However, the changing pattern of adult relationships, and in particular the breakdown of so many married and unmarried partnerships, has been a major factor in the law becoming increasingly, involved with children. One out of every five children in this country is being brought up by a single parent. Countless numbers of children are being brought up in homes where one of the parental figures is not their natural parent.

The Child's Voice

Children themselves had very little, if any, say in decision making about what should happen to them. Until fairly recently, as far as the law was concerned, children were, of course, children until they reached the age of eighteen. Decisions were made over their heads, without anyone giving any particular thought to their age or maturity, or considering that they might have a right to a say, in the decision making process.

Professionals concerned with children – lawyers, social workers and child psychologists among them – recognised the problems. Why should parents not be given more responsibility for deciding what should happen to their own children? Why should the court have to become involved if they can reach agreement between themselves? Why should the children themselves, depending on their age and understanding, not be given a real voice when what was to happen to them was being discussed?

Laws have had to be made relating to disputes between parents and others about where, and with whom, children should live, and with whom and in what circumstances they should have contact. Laws have had to be made to deal with financial support for the carers of children.

In 1989 the Children Act was passed in an effort to tackle these problems and others. For the first time, all the law relating to children had been brought together. 'Custody' and 'access' old-fashioned legal words which had become so emotive, were to be replaced by the more neutral terms 'residence' and 'contact'.

One of the more horrific aspects of life in our society today is that so many children suffer from abuse and neglect. Abuse can be physical or emotional. Over the last twenty years the problem of abuse of children appears to have increased, particularly with regard to sexual abuse. Whatever the reasons for this, and they are many and complex, the law has had to intervene to try to protect children.

Family breakdown, coupled with the need to protect children from abuse and neglect, has meant that a growing number of children have had to be cared for away from their own families. Laws have had to be made about how children should be looked after when, for some reason, their own families cannot cope, and they need to be fostered, adopted or put into local authority care. (For further information on this see Chapters 10 and 11.)

Over the last hundred years the emphasis has completely shifted from parental rights to parental responsibility. One of the most important things to realise about parental responsibility is that it can be shared equally by the mother and the father, even after they have separated or been divorced. In the past, if one parent had been granted a custody order, the other parent often felt excluded from the child's life or, at best, marginalised.

Custody is an outdated notion. Since the law relating to children was reformed, the parent with whom the child will be living is given a residence order. If the parents agree about where the child should live there is no need for the court to make any order at all.

CASE STUDY

William's mother has obtained a residence order from the court which says that he is to live with her. William's father has been granted a contact order, which sets out the periods which William will spend with him. But these orders do not in any way lessen the parental responsibility of William's father who can exercise his parental responsibility in any way he thinks best in William's interests, whenever William is visiting him.

Both parents should feel that each has an equal opportunity to take part in decision making about the upbringing of their child and that they are equally responsible for their child, whoever happens to have the residence order. Parental responsibility enables a parent to take part in decisions about the important things which are to happen in the child's life.

In the past, because children were looked on as little more than the possessions of their parents, the law tended to enforce the 'rights' of parents over the children. In fact, not all that long ago, it was only the father who had rights; the mother had none at all. For example, it was not uncommon for a mother who had been found to have committed adultery to be refused any future contact with her child by the court. But if mothers were given no rights over their children, the children were in an even worse position.

Pity poor Harriet, whose mother had left her father for very good reasons in 1878. The father took Harriet and her brothers and sisters away from their mother with the full approval with the court. The eldest child was twelve years old. The father could not look after them himself so he boarded them out with 'clergymen and other persons . . . in many and various places'. He permitted their mother to visit them only once every month, and he insisted that any letters written to the mother by the children, and from the mother to the children, had to be censored.

Harriet must have been a brave girl. When she was sixteen she wrote to the judge and asked him to allow her to live with her mother. If she could not live with her, would the judge allow Harriet to spend a holiday with her ? Her letter was a sad one. 'Father has no place to take me to, and with one exception has never spent a vacation with us over four years. I am almost always among strangers. I am longing to see some of my relations,' she wrote.

But when her request came to be considered by the court, it was decided that the court had no power to interfere with the legal right of a father to have absolute control over his children and to decide where they should live and who they should see.

Contrast what happened to poor Harriet and her mother with what happened almost exactly a hundred years later, when Mrs Victoria Gillick, the mother of five girls, attempted to persuade a court that advice on contraception should not be given to her daughters while they were under the age of sixteen, unless she, as their mother, had agreed that such advice could be given.

The House of Lords decided that Mrs Gillick did not have complete control over her children. It said that the rights of a parent come from the parent's duty to protect the child. But the child has rights too. As a child grew older and more intelligent and mature, the rights of the child increased. In other words, a child who is old enough, and intelligent enough, to understand what it is to be decided and what the consequences of a decision will be, must be allowed to make his or her own choice. As the child grows in maturity and intelligence so the right of the parents to make decisions about the child gradually dwindles away. Mrs Gillick's right to choose whether or not her child could have certain medical advice would come to an end if, and when, each child was intelligent enough to understand what the choice was and what the consequences were likely to be. So this case paved the way for the child's right to a voice in decisions to be made about him or her by the courts.

There is a checklist for the court which sets out the matters which have to be considered in any case about children. The full checklist is given later in this chapter. But what is interesting is that the very first item for the court to consider which is set out in the checklist is 'the ascertainable wishes and feelings of the child . . . considered in the light of (his or her) age and understanding'.

Family lawyers can tell you from experience that the wishes and feelings of almost every child involved in any court proceedings where parents are in conflict are sadly predictable. Occasionally, in special circumstances, a judge will agree to see the children during a case where their future is under discussion. This does not happen very often, because the judge will usually have the assistance of a report from the court welfare officer. When a judge decides to see them, the children will be brought to a private room, away from the court itself. The argument between the parents may be about with which of them the children are to live. The judge will talk to the children without either parent, or their legal representatives, being present in the room.

The judge then comes back into court, having talked to the children, to explain to the parents what the children have said. Almost always the judge will say that the children have said that they want only that their mother and father should live together again, without any arguments. The judge will point out that this is one order which the court cannot make. He or she will then go on to do the best that can be done if the parents have decided that they cannot go on together and cannot even agree about what should happen to their children.

Will a Court always Order what the Children want?

Great importance is now given to the wishes and feelings of children, but what a child wants cannot always be the end of the matter. For example, there was a recent case where a child of twelve was described by a judge as 'fixed and determined' in her desire to live with her father. But the judge then went on to say that the child was too young to carry the burden of decisions about her own future. He said that she must be told, with appropriate sympathy and firmness, that the decision and the responsibility for it had to be taken for her. She would be sad, the judge thought, but she must be helped to make the best of it.

This does not mean that every twelve year old would be considered too young to make decisions. For example, the wishes of a twelve year old about whether or not to have contact with someone might be quite decisive. Children do mature at different rates and one girl of twelve may be quite childish still, while her friend of exactly the same age might be quite mature and responsible. The court tries to assess the intelligence and understanding of the individual child in each case, rather than taking some arbitrary rule of thumb based on age alone.

Does the Court have to Make an Order about a Child?

As a matter of fact, the court need not make any order at all if it considers that this would be better for the child concerned. This 'leave well alone' idea is a new one. Before the Children Act was passed, an order would always be made by the court if an application about a child had been made. The order would be made even if the case had been settled by agreement. In every divorce case where there were children of the family, the court had to make custody and access orders even if there was no dispute about what should happen. This minimised the responsibility of the parents. The new approach underlines the fact that it is the parents who have the primary responsibility where decisions have to be made about the future of their children.

From the child's point of view, how much happier it will make him or her to be told that the mother and father have taken the decision about what is to happen together, rather than becoming aware that an almighty court battle is taking place, with an order having to be made which will leave one parent a 'winner' and the other a 'loser'.

There are four separate and equally important things which any judge must bear in mind when dealing with a case concerning a child.

1. The welfare of the child is paramount in deciding all questions about the child.

2. Delay, in deciding any question about a child's upbringing is likely to prejudice the child's welfare.

3. There is a checklist (see below) of matters to which the court has to pay particular attention.

4. The court should not make an order unless to do so is considered better for the child than making no order,

The Checklist

The court has to pay particular attention to the following matters, set out in the Act and described as 'the checklist':

(a) the ascertainable wishes and feelings of the child concerned (considered in the light of his age and understanding);

(b) the physical, emotional and educational needs of the child;

(c) the likely effect upon the child of any change in the circumstances of the child;

(d) the age, sex and background of the child and any other characteristics of the child which the court considers relevant;

(e) any harm which the child has suffered or which the child may be at risk of suffering;

(f) how capable each of the child's parents, and any other person in relation to whom the court considers the question to be relevant, is of meeting his or her needs;

(g) the range of powers available to the court under the Act in the proceedings before it.

Welfare

Some of these matters need a little further explanation. What exactly is 'welfare', for example?

One judge has said this:

> '"Welfare" is an all-encompassing word. It includes material welfare, both in the sense of adequacy of resources to provide a pleasant home and a comfortable standard of living and in the sense of adequacy of care to ensure that good health and due personal pride are maintained. However, while material considerations have their place they are secondary matters.
>
> More important are the stability and security, the loving and understanding care and guidance, the warm and compassionate relationships, that are essential for the full development of the child's own character, personality and talents.'

It would be hard to find a better way of describing the welfare principle.

Delay

Most parents would wholeheartedly agree that delay in deciding some dispute about a child, with which of them the child is to live for example, can have very serious effects on the child, quite apart from the worry, disappointment, and frustration experienced by the parents.

In the past, cases would often drag on for weeks, months, even years. Solicitors often have very heavy caseloads. Some solicitors are less efficient than others. It could, and did, happen that cases concerning children were put on the back burner because other matters seemed more urgent or important.

To parents, or other concerned people, delay in deciding some question about a child can be infuriating. There were many cases in which the single factor of delay really forced the court into a decision which would not have been taken if the matter could have come before the court reasonably promptly.

CASE STUDY

Four year old Billy had been placed with long-term foster parents for over a year before the application by his parents to have him returned came to court. The court was faced with the problem that the parents, who might otherwise have been able to have Billy returned to them, were now almost strangers as far as he was concerned. To uproot him from the family he viewed as his own, would have caused great and possibly irreparable harm. So the court, in Billy's interest, would have to refuse the parents' application.

Cases such as Billy's resulted in the new system under the Children Act. This requires the court to make orders to keep cases moving along, to set dates by which certain procedures should be carried out, and to make sure that solicitors have a timetable which they must be careful to keep.

How is the Act Working?

The many new provisions of the Children Act have only been in force for a relatively short time. Obviously, there have been teething troubles but it certainly has achieved some of its objectives. Parents are thinking more about responsibility than their 'rights'. Children's voices are being heard. Cases about children are, on the whole, coming to court faster.

Few, if any, family lawyers would want to go back to the situation before the Act came into force.

CHAPTER FIVE

PARENTAL RESPONSIBILITY

Parental 'rights' have disappeared and have been replaced by what the law calls parental responsibility, i.e. the obligations of any parent to care for his or her own child. What are these responsibilities of parenthood?

When you come to think about it the responsibilities of a parent are actually changing all the time, as the child develops. It would be difficult, if not impossible, to compile a comprehensive list of them because the contents of the list would change from month to month and from year to year as the child grew up. The parents of a new-born baby have quite different responsibilities from those which they have when their baby has become a teenager. It might be possible to list all the responsibilities of a parent at one particular stage in a child's life, but the responsibilities on that list would be the ones for that stage and would constantly have to be changed as the child became more independent and more able to take decisions for itself. And you can't just rely on the child's age – the responsibilities on you as a parent at a particular point in time will depend on all kinds of variable factors – no child develops at exactly the same rate and in exactly the same ways as any other.

So it is difficult to attempt to define exactly what parental responsibility is. I suppose the best definition is that it includes a duty to do whatever seems to be in the best interests of your child at whatever stage he or she is in life.

Who has Parental Responsibility?

When the mother and father of a child are married to each other at the date of the child's birth, each will automatically have parental responsibility for that child. The parental responsibility will not be

taken from one or the other parent as a result of divorce or separation. If you, or your ex, have been given custody of a child before the
1989 Children Act, that does not mean that the other parent has lost
his or her parental responsibility.

If a mother and father are not married at the date of the child's
birth, but were married at any time during the period when the mother
was pregnant with the child, the father still gets parental responsibility on the birth of the child. Even if the baby was the result of artificial insemination the position would still be the same.

If the mother and father are not married, the father will not automatically get parental responsibility. Only the mother will have parental responsibility on the birth of the child, unless there is a parental responsibility agreement or a parental responsibility order is made
by the court.

CASE STUDY

Sophie's parents are Andrew and Jill. When Sophie was
conceived Andrew and Jill were married. Sadly, they divorced two months before Sophie's birth. Andrew and Jill
will both have parental responsibility for Sophie, even though
they had ceased to be married before she was born.

CASE STUDY

Gary and Sue have a son called Michael. When Michael was
conceived Gary and Sue were not married to one another,
but they married during Sue's pregnancy. Both Sue and Gary
automatically acquired parental responsibility when Michael
was born.

If you are an Unmarried Father can you get Parental Responsibility?

CASE STUDY

Richard and Jane have never been married. They have a
daughter, Elizabeth. Jane, as the mother, acquired immedi-
ate parental responsibility when Elizabeth was born. Richard,

like many unmarried fathers, wants to play a full part in the
life of his little girl, even though he and her mother are not
married. How can he get parental responsibility for Elizabeth?

There are a number of ways in which fathers, like Richard can acquire parental responsibility.

1. If Jane agrees that Richard should have all the legal responsibili-
    ties of a father, she can enter into a formal agreement with him
    that he should have parental responsibility. As a result of that
    formal agreement, Richard will acquire parental responsibility
    for Elizabeth without any necessity to go to court to ask for an
    order.

    This is known as a parental responsibility agreement. Both
    the mother and the father must sign the form, which is then filled
    at court. You can get the form from your local county court of-
    fice.

2. If a court had already granted Richard custody or care and con-
    trol over Elizabeth under the old law, that order would have given
    him parental responsibility.

3. If Richard has not been granted an order for custody or care and
    control of Elizabeth under the old law, and if Jane does not agree
    that he should have parental responsibility, Richard can apply to
    the court for a parental responsibility order.

4. Richard might think that it would be in Elizabeth's best interests
    to live with him, rather than with her mother. In those circum-
    stances, he could apply for a residence order (which used to be
    called a custody order). If the court decided to grant him a resi-
    dence order, he would automatically acquire parental responsi-
    bility.

How does the Court Decide
about giving Parental Responsibility?

The court will, generally, make a parental responsibilty order in favour of the father, unless there are exceptional circumstances. How-

ever, the court always has to think about what would be in the best interests of the child concerned. So Richard's application for a parental responsibility order will be considered in the light of what would be in Elizabeth's best interests. Elizabeth's own wishes and feelings will be taken into account, if she is old enough to understand what her father's application means. Her physical, emotional and educational needs will also be considered, as will the likely effect on her of any order made as a result of Richard's application. Her age, sex and background will be relevant. There may be other things about her which the court will consider relevant too. The court must also consider whether Elizabeth has suffered, or is likely to suffer, any harm as a result of Richard's application or of any order which might be made.

For example, suppose that Richard had another daughter whom he had seriously abused. The court might well decide that there could be a risk that he might similarly abuse Elizabeth. In those circumstances, it might well refuse to grant the parental responsibility order.

It is very likely that the court would request the help of a court welfare officer before making a decision about Richard's application. The welfare officer would make enquiries and talk to everyone concerned in order to be able to provide the judge with information about Elizabeth and her parents and background. What a court welfare officer does is fully explained in Chapter 8.

Some matters which will be important when the court considers a father's application are:

(a) the degree of commitment which the father has shown towards the child;

(b) the degree of attachment which exists between the father and the child;

(c) the father's reasons for applying for the order.

For example, if Richard had shown little or no real interest in Elizabeth up until the time when he made his application to the court, the court might be reluctant to make a parental responsibility order in his favour.

Again, if Elizabeth has had contact with Richard but without becoming fond of him, Richard's case for a parental responsibility order might be a weaker one. However, it has to be said that if Elizabeth's mother Jane has consistently obstructed contact, so that there has been no possibility of Elizabeth forming an attachment to Richard, his application might still succeed if he could show that it would be in Elizabeth's interests to form a relationship with him.

Richard's reasons for applying for the order will be very important. It is not unknown, unfortunately, for a father to make an application about a child simply in order to interfere in the life of the mother or to avenge himself for some former hurt. If the court were to take the view that Richard had some such motivation, this might be fatal to his application.

In Richard's case, as with every other case where a parent makes an application about a child, his interests as a father will not override what the court considers to be in the best interests of Elizabeth. You might think that this was so obviously the correct approach that the courts of any civilised country would take the same view.

Surprisingly, not all legal systems put the interests of the child first.

CASE STUDY

> In a recent American case, for example, a little girl who had been adopted as a baby was taken away at the age of two and a half from the only parents she had ever really known. Sobbing for her 'mommy', she was strapped into a child's seat in her natural father's car and driven off. That father was a stranger so far as the child was concerned, but his rights were allowed to predominate.
>
> Television cameras recorded the child's distress and bewilderment. Her mother, when agreeing to the adoption, had lied about the identity of the father. That resulted in a legal situation where the father's 'rights' were the most important consideration, whatever the resultant trauma to a toddler might be.

But putting the child's interests first, does not mean that decisions about giving parental responsibility to someone, Richard for example, are easy ones for the court to make.

However, had the little American girl been a child adopted in this country, it is unlikely that a judge would have made an order which had the effect of uprooting her from adoptive parents, with whom she was happy and settled, to place her in the care of the father whom she did not know.

Divorced or Separated Parents

CASE STUDY

Carl was four years old. His parents had separated when he was three months old. His father had made no attempt to keep in contact with him, he had paid no maintenance for him nor had he ever sent presents, cards or letters at times such as birthdays or Christmas. Eventually, however, his father had applied for access (now called contact) with Carl.

By the time his father's application came before the court, Carl was three and a half. The first judge granted access initially to take place in the presence of a court welfare officer. Carl's mother appealed. She had remarried and made a new life for herself and her son. She viewed the prospect of Carl's introduction to his father as nothing less than a disaster.

So far as Carl himself was concerned, he believed that his mother's new husband was his daddy. His mother's anxiety about his father's proposed entry into Carl's life was such that it was bound to be sensed by Carl. The relationship between Carl's mother and his stepfather would also be placed under strain. That strain would inevitably affect Carl himself.

The appeal judges asked themselves what good the father could do Carl. The answer was none. What harm could he do him? The answer was, possibly, a great deal. To take Carl to meet his father, who was a stranger to him, seemed a horrifying idea. The court went on to talk about the pain and anguish which would be caused to Carl's mother, her parents and her second husband by the introduction of Carl to his father.

The test was said to be whether starting access now, after this long lapse of time, would be of any positive benefit to Carl.

All three of the judges who heard the appeal understood that the judge who made the access order had been guided by the principle that children ought to know their fathers.

> While agreeing with that principle in theory, they consid-
> ered that the circumstances of that particular little boy were
> such that his interests overrode the principle.

Although this particular case was decided before the Children Act was passed, the approach taken by the appeal judges in the case could still serve as a guideline to judges considering applications for parental responsibility by fathers who had not had contact with their children for a long time.

It must be stressed that every case depends upon its own facts. It is certainly not true that contact or a parental responsibility order will always be refused where there has been a gap in contact between father and child, nor will it invariably be refused when the mother has made a new relationship, but these factors will undoubtedly be given weight when the court has to make a decision about introducing an unknown father into the life of his child, and particularly where the child has no idea that he has any father but the one who lives with his mother.

Where parents who have been married are separated or divorced, each of them will continue to have parental responsibility. This means that a parent who does not have a child living with him or her should still be treated as a parent by, for example, the child's school. In the past, when a custody order had been made in favour of one parent, head teachers of the children's schools all too frequently behaved as though the children had only one parent.

In such situations, the parent who did not have care and control would receive no copies of school reports and no invitations to parents' evenings or school functions. Not every school took this line, of course, but it was certainly not uncommon.

Any parent who was marginalised by the child's school in this way was bound to feel upset and frustration. The Law Commission which considered the concept of parental responsibility prior to the Children Act, emphasised in its report that a parent who does not have the child living with him or her should still be regarded in law as a parent. It was specifically pointed out that such parents should be treated as parents by schools and given information and an opportunity to take part in the education of their children.

Some head teachers would make the excuse that, because they

were providing the custodial parent with reports and information, they expected that parent to pass everything on to the other parent. In an ideal world, one night expect that sort of co-operation between parents no longer living together. Unfortunately, in the real world the head teachers were often being overly optimistic.

Exercising Parental Responsibility

Parental responsibility can be exercised independently by a parent when the child is in his or her care, whether or not that parent has a residence order. However, there are certain limitations to this and it can be a tricky area.

CASE STUDY

> Sarah and Tom are the divorced parents of Luke. A residence order has been made in favour of Sarah. Luke attends a school in the area of his home with Sarah. The school does not accept a certain style of haircut and will exclude any boy with that hairstyle.
> Luke is having weekend staying contact with Tom. Can Tom decide to exercise his parental responsibility by having Luke's hair cut in the style forbidden by the school?

This can be seen as an example of an attempt to exercise parental responsibility by Tom which would be incompatible with the court order that Luke reside with his mother. Consequently, it would not be appropriate for Tom to exercise his parental responsibilities in this way, Not many fathers would want to do something likely to have their child excluded from school, so it is to hoped that this situation would not arise too frequently!

But suppose, during that same weekend, Tom decided to take Luke to a sporting event of which he knew Sarah would disapprove? It would probably be a perfectly proper exercise of Tom's parental responsibility for him to take the decision to bring Luke to the event, even though aware of Sarah's disapproval.

Again, these are examples only. For the sake of Luke's peace of mind, one would hope that Tom and Sarah could reach some agreement about the sporting event to enable Luke to enjoy it without any feeling of guilt about upsetting his mother.

There are some aspects of a child's life which are so fundamentally important that a parent with parental responsibility cannot take a decision about them without the agreement of the other parent with responsibility. For example, whether a child should have an operation or not would usually be a matter for both parents, unless it was an emergency situation. What school a child should attend is also a question which should be jointly decided by both parents. When parents cannot agree on an issue of this kind, either of them can apply to the court for a judge to make a decision. A parent cannot take a child out of the country permanently without the consent of the other parent from an order of the court, and the consent of each parent with responsibility would be required before an adoption order could be made in respect of a child unless the court dispensed with that consent.

When Someone Else Acquires Parental Responsibility

Step-parents

What happens if Sarah remarries and she and her new husband Charles obtain residence orders in respect of Luke? Charles acquires parental responsibility for Luke because of the residence order, but Tom does not lose his parental responsibility. This means that more than two parents can have parental responsibility for the same child.

Children in Care

When a care order is made in respect of a child, or when an emergency protection order is taken out, parental responsibility is conferred on the local authority. But the natural parents, with parental responsibility, do not lose it as a result of a care order or emergency protection order, although they will be limited in what they can do.

Adoption

An adoption order confers parental responsibility on the adoptive parent or parents. It terminates the parental responsibility of the natural parents. Adoption will be considered in detail in Chapter 10. It is important to remember however, that foster parents do not acquire parental responsibility.

Guardians

Guardians are the people appointed, usually by parents, to look after a child in the event of a parent's death.

Anyone with parental responsibility can appoint someone to be a child's guardian in the event of death. Before the Children Act a parent could only appoint a guardian by executing a legal document called a deed, or by making a will. But it is now sufficient if the appointment is made in writing, is dated and is signed by the person making it.

A parent with parental responsibility can appoint a guardian to replace him or her in the event of death. However, if the parent, who makes the appointment, does not have a residence order, the appointment will not take effect unless and until the parent with the residence order dies too.

All parents should think seriously about what they would wish to happen to their children in the event of their death. If you choose a guardian for your children you must, of course, consult that person about whether he or she would be willing to accept the responsibility. Once you have chosen the guardian, there is no need to do anything other than record your wish in writing, date it and sign it. It is advisable to seek legal advice in case there are any unforeseen complications. Also you must ensure that the document is kept in a safe and secure place, and can be found easily in the event of death.

If you are making a will – and everyone should – the appointment of the guardian could be included in that.

The court can appoint someone as the guardian of a child, when no appointment has been made by a parent, in two situations.

1. Michael's parents are dead so no one has parental responsibility for him. The court can appoint a guardian for Michael, who will be given parental responsibility, on his or her appointment.

2. Jennifer lived with her mother Patricia, who had been granted a residence order. Jennifer's father has taken no interest in her for

several years. Sadly, Patricia has died of cancer. The court can appoint a guardian for Jennifer and the guardian will have parental responsibility.

It seems that any relative or family friend could apply to be appointed the guardian of a child for whom no one has parental responsibility. In theory, it would appear that a child could apply to the court for a guardian to be appointed if the child is of sufficient maturity to understand the application.

A guardian who is appointed by the court to have parental responsibility for a child should not be confused with a *guardian ad litem*, someone appointed by the court to represent a child in proceedings before the court. The responsibilities of a *guardian ad litem* are limited and usually consist of representing a child in specific legal proceedings.

When does Parental Responsibility End?

All parental responsibility ends when the child is eighteen years old. Where the child's parents have never been married and the father has acquired parental responsibility by means of a court order, or through the formal consent of the mother, the order or agreement ends automatically once the child reaches the age of eighteen.

The court can also make an order that parental responsibility should end, if it has been acquired by court order or by agreement. An order terminating parental responsibility in such a case can be made on the application of someone with parental responsibility for the child (which will include the father himself). An order terminating parental responsibility can also be made on the application of the child, with the permission of the court. As with any application made by a child, the court will first have to satisfy itself that the child has sufficient understanding to make the application.

CHAPTER SIX

WHAT SHOULD WE DO
ABOUT THE CHILDREN?

When parents split up, their children are in the front line. If the children are of an age where they still need parental care, the first question to be answered is where and with whom they are going to live. Tied up with that decision are the questions about how often and for how long they will see the parent with whom they are not living.

Any breakdown in a relationship is going to be traumatic for the couple concerned. If they have been sufficiently committed to one another to have children, it is almost inevitable that the trauma of the breakdown will be correspondingly greater. Far too often children get caught in the crossfire because parents are too occupied with their own feelings of hurt and rejection to think clearly.

No loving parent would willingly inflict emotional pain on a child, but when coping with the turmoil of separation and loss a parent can be blinded to what should be obvious.

Divorce and Separation:
Children have a Right to Know

Children, even very young children, are only too aware of any tension in the relationship between their parents. The story is told of the couple who resolved that their small son and daughter would never be given a hint of any disagreement between them. When they were irritated with one another they took particular care to be even more polite than usual. They prided themselves on their success in concealing their quarrels, until the day when they had to use physical force to separate their squabbling children. The little boy pointed at his sister and said accusingly, 'She called me "darling" first!'

That story illustrates precisely what so often happens. Parents may believe that their children have no idea that there are any problems between them. But it is in fact rare for children of a floundering relationship not to realise that one or both of their parents is feeling unhappy, or that something is wrong.

Some parents find the temptation to enlist the sympathy of the children irresistible. But most children love their parents equally. Children certainly need both parents. The fact that the parental relationship has broken down should not mean that they lose out any more than they must.

Parents who have decided to separate should try to explain to their children exactly what is happening. If at all possible they should explain to the children together. The words they use will obviously depend upon the ages of the children, but even the smallest children deserve to be given some explanation which they can understand.

Child psychiatrists who have made a study of the children of divorced or separated parents have come up with some surprising conclusions. For example, they have discovered that children often believe that the breakdown of their parents' relationship is somehow their fault. It needs to be carefully explained to a child that adults do stop loving one another sometimes. Equally, it should be emphasised that both parents still love the child, and will not stop doing so whatever happens.

Child experts have also found that, if a parent leaves home and there is no careful explanation given to small children, they will worry desperately about the possibility that the parent who is still there will vanish too. The child's reasoning is: if Daddy can go away, so might Mummy. Who will look after me then?

That might seem laughable to an adult, but for the child who does not understand what has happened or why, and to whom no one attempts to explain what has happened, the logic is remorseless.

Small children can feel great anxiety about the parent who leaves. Where will he or she sleep? Who will cook their meals? If there is no discussion about the parent's plans, a child may suffer acute and quite unnecessary concern, and this will be in addition to the unavoidable distress caused by the breakdown itself. To see for itself where the absent parent will be living helps the child to come to terms with the new situation.

Some parents feel that talking to their children about the breakdown of their relationship is simply too difficult. But if the children are given no explanation of what is happening in their lives they are likely to be very frightened and confused.

Fortunately, there are now many organisations which are able to help with counselling for parents at times like this. This counselling is called 'conciliation' but parents should not be put off by this word. It is often mistakenly thought to mean 'reconciliation', in other words an attempt to patch up a failed relationship. Conciliation recognises that the relationship has broken down. Counsellors work with the parents to find the best solutions to the practical problems thrown up by the breakdown. There is a list of helpful organisations at the end of this chapter.

Custody, Care and Control, and Access

Before the Children Act came into force in 1991, most people were familiar with the ideas of custody, care and control, and access. Parents could even have a joint custody order, which gave care and control to one or other of them. Joint custody orders were not all that common, since the court had to be convinced that the parents could work together harmoniously for the good of a child before such an order could be made. More usual were orders which gave sole custody, care and control to one parent.

In either case, the parent who did not have care and control could be granted access – visiting access or staying (overnight) access, or both. In rare cases, a parent would not be given access, or would have access limited to sending letters, cards and gifts.

'Custody', 'care' and 'control' were emotive words. The non-custodial parent frequently felt excluded from a child's life. The word 'access' appeared to imply that the child somehow 'belonged' to the parent who had care and control. The word 'custody' appeared to confirm that idea.

The mere fact that whenever a divorce took place there had to be a court order about what should happen to the children often gave rise to difficulties where there should have been none. For example, it was not unusual for separating parents to be in complete agreement about what should happen in relation to their children. But the court still had to intervene by making an order, even though it would be expressed to be 'by consent'.

There was always some confusion about the extent of the right of the parent who did not have custody to be consulted about important decisions in the life of a child – whether or not the child should have some operation in hospital, for example, or which school should be chosen, or which religion the child should be taught. Where parents were not on the best of terms following a split, the tendency might be for the custodial parent to make all the decisions without consulting the other parent at all. This sort of thing would inevitably upset the other parent – and, of course, the child! A parent like this was, consciously or unconsciously, using the child as a weapon in an ongoing conflict with the other parent.

The courts tried to give guidance about this and insisted that a custody order did not give the custodial parent absolute rights over all decision making about the child. Attempts were sometimes made to overcome the difficulty by granting joint custody orders, in order to emphasise that both parents shared responsibility. However, most judges would only agree to make a joint custody order if they could be satisfied that the parents were able to relate to one another reasonably and to make decisions together. This meant that in the cases where there was most acrimony it was more likely that a sole custody order would be made, giving one parent the power to use the child as a weapon against the other.

It was in order to bring parents back to the realisation that each has equal responsibility for his or her child that custody orders were abolished to be replaced by the – hopefully neutral – residence orders.

However, the old orders still exist, side by side with the new residence and contact orders. Where orders were made before the Children Act came into force, they remain as custody, care and control, and access orders unless or until they are varied by the court on the application of either parent, or even by the child concerned.

New Words for Old?

Child psychiatrists and other experts agree that the children with separated parents each of whom encourages them to love the other parent survive the breakdown of their parents' relationship best.

Laws cannot be passed to compel parents to be nice to one another, to put their own hurts aside, and to encourage their children to love the parent who may have behaved badly as a partner. But it was realised that the orders which were being made before the Children Act were actually working against parental co-operation. Parents thought of themselves as being 'winners' or 'losers' when it came to orders relating to children. The parent with care and control had won. The parent with access had lost.

The thinking behind the Children Act was to try to avoid this kind of unnecessary emotional distress for parents as far as possible. The emphasis is now placed firmly on the idea of parental responsibility. Each parent has equal parental responsibility, whenever the child is with him or her. The very words 'custody' and 'access' had become so loaded with emotive overtones that it was decided that the Act should do away with them.

The Choices for the Court

The court now has three choices when faced with the problem of what should happen to the children on the breakdown of a marriage.

1. To make no order at all

This is now the preferred option, and one which was simply not open to the court prior to the Children Act. It underlines the fact that each parent has responsibility for the child. The parents are obviously the best people to make decisions about their child. If they can do so, it should be left to them, and the court should not intervene. Children themselves will be much happier if they feel that their parents have come to a joint decision about what is to happen to them.

For these reasons, parents are very much encouraged by the law to make their own decisions if at all possible. Many agencies have been set up to try to help parents to discuss the future arrangements for their children and to reach an amicable and mutually agreed plan. The court's own conciliation process, which will be discussed in Chapter 7, is another area where help may be found.

2. To make a residence order in favour of one parent and a contact order in favour of the other

Unfortunately, where parents cannot agree, it has to be admitted that this kind of order will all too frequently be seen by them in the old winning/losing terms. The mere change of wording seldom helps in reality. If there is a court battle, as a result of which one parent gains a residence order, it matters little to the other parent that it is no longer described as custody, care and control.

3. To make a split residence order

This is an order which means that the child resides with one parent for part of the week, month or year, and with the other for the remainder of the week, month or year. Courts may be tempted to make such orders to avoid giving the impression that one parent has won and the other lost, but these order are unusual. The problem with a split residence order is that it is generally better for a child to know where his or her home is. Dividing the child's time more or less equally between two parents can result in a lack of security and permanence for the child, whatever the satisfaction for the parents.

Other Orders the Court can Make

The court has been given power to make two completely new orders regarding children.

1. Prohibited steps orders

These orders are made when the court wants to limit the parental responsibility of a parent in some specific way.

CASE STUDY

In an earlier chapter, Sarah and Tom, the parents of Luke, were discussed. A residence order has been made in favour of Sarah. Luke attends a school near his home with Sarah. The school does not accept a certain style of haircut and will exclude any boy with that hairstyle.

Luke is going to have weekend staying contact with Tom, who has told Sarah that he intends to exercise his parental responsibility by having Luke's hair cut in the style banned by the school. Sarah can apply to the court for a prohibited steps order, forbidding Tom to exercise his parental responsibility by having Luke's hair cut in that particular hairstyle.

2. Specific issue order

These orders are made when there is some specific matter of dispute between parents which they cannot resolve by agreement.

CASE STUDY

Tom has decided that the school attended by Luke is run by a reactionary authoritarian head teacher. He wants Luke to change to another local school where hairstyles are a matter of choice. Sarah, on the other hand, is happy with Luke's present school and wishes him to continue there. Either Sarah or Tom can apply to the court to decide on the question of which school Luke should attend. This kind of application results in a specific issue order, when the court settles the matter although, it is of course to be hoped that parent can resolve this sort of dispute between themselves, without having to make an application to the court.

Who may Apply for Orders?

1. Residence, contact, prohibited steps or specific issue orders

(a) Any parent can apply, this includes unmarried fathers;

(b) Any guardian can apply;

(c) Any person with a residence order can apply.

2. Residence or contact orders only

(a) Anyone listed under (1) above;

(b) Anyone married to the parent of a child, who has treated the child as 'a child of the family', has the right to apply, even if the marriage has ended;

(c) Anyone with whom a child has lived for a period of at least three years has the right to apply;

(d) Anyone who has the consent of each person with a residence order in respect of the child can apply;

(e) If the child is in the care of a local authority under a care order, anyone with the consent of the local authority can apply;

(f) In any other case each person with parental responsibility for a child is entitled to apply.

3. Other people

Anyone who is not entitled to make an application under any of the categories set out above may apply to the court for permission to make an application. This includes the child, who may be granted permission if he is considered to be of sufficient understanding and maturity.

Grandparents, and other interested relatives or friends of the child, can also apply for permission to make an application, if they do not qualify under any of the categories listed above. There will usually be little difficulty in obtaining permission for anyone who can show that it would be in a child's interests for an order to be made.

Effect of Residence Orders

1. Change of child's surname

If you are considering changing your child's surname, do be aware that it is an automatic condition of all residence orders that you have to get the written consent of every person with parental responsibility for the child, or the permission of the court. The court will, in certain circumstances, give permission for a child's surname to be changed, even where one of the child's parents is opposed to the change.

Changing a child's surname is something which should not be done lightly. A court would need to be satisfied that the change is going to be in the interests of the child.

CASE STUDY

Jemma R's parents divorced and her mother remarried. The new husband was Mr T. Her mother allowed Jemma to be known as Jemma T by friends and neighbours, and registered her at school as 'Jemma R known as T'. Mr R objected to his daughter being known by the new surname. Jemma's mother applied to the court for leave to change the child's surname.

It was decided that it would not be in Jemma's interests, and would be totally unrealistic, for the court to make an order forbidding the use of the mother's new surname by Jemma. The order would be impossible to enforce. Jemma knew that her real surname was R, but all her friends and schoolteachers called her Jemma T. The court held that it would not be in her interests to have the name by which she was already known changed to her real name.

This case was decided in the early 1980s. Although one can understand the reasoning behind the decision, it should not be taken as an encouragement to mothers to defy the law, which now makes it clear that a child's surname may not be changed without the consent of the other parent or the leave of the court.

A change of surname is a question on which a child might have views of his or her own. In such a case, if the child were to be of sufficient maturity and understanding, the court might grant leave for the child to make an application about a change of surname.

2. Taking a child out of the country

Where a residence order is in force, no person may remove the child from the United Kingdom without either the written consent of every person with parental responsibility, or the permission of the court.

However, a person who has a residence order may remove the

child for a period of less than one month. This is to enable people with residence orders to take children abroad for the purpose of normal holidays.

It sometimes happens that a parent suspects that the parent with the residence order intends to take the child abroad permanently, rather than simply for a holiday. In such a case, the anxious parent can apply for a prohibited steps order, forbidding the parent with the residence order from removing the child.

If the court is satisfied that there is a real risk that the child will not be returned it can make the prohibited steps order.

3. Conditions attached to orders

If the court considers it to be in the interests of a child, it can attach a condition or conditions to a residence order. For example, if the court considered that there was a real risk of a parent with residence taking the child abroad permanently, the court could attach a condition to the residence order to minimise the risk. The condition might be that the parent with residence was not to remove the child from the jurisdiction for any period without the permission of the court or the consent of the other parent.

Family Assistance Orders

Behind all the provisions of the Children Act is the hope that parents will be able to co-operate with one another for the sake of their children. Lawyers and other professionals concerned with families are only too aware of the strength of feeling which exists when relationships have broken down.

Sometimes it is just too much to expect that emotions will cool immediately when disputes have had to be resolved by court proceedings. The win/lose view is likely to persist. The temptation to use the children as weapons in an ongoing conflict between the parents can be irresistible, and can have disastrous results for the children.

For this reason, the courts have been empowered to make family assistance orders. These orders require that a probation officer or local authority social worker should be made available to 'advise, assist and (where appropriate) befriend any person named in the order'. Social workers have had rather a bad press in recent years, and parents sometimes become alarmed at the suggestion that a social worker should be involved with them and their children. But in the case of family assistance orders, social workers are there to do just that, assist. Their training enables them to sort out areas of difficulty.

People who may be named in a family assistance order are:

(a) any parent (including an unmarried father);

(b) any guardian;

(c) any person with whom the child is living;

(d) any person in whose favour a contact order is in force;

(e) any child.

Family assistance orders may only be made if the court believes that the circumstances of the case are 'exceptional'. The court must also be satisfied that the consent of every person named in the order (other than the child) has been obtained to the making of the order.

Family assistance orders are intended to be a temporary assistance in situations where parents, or other interested parties, find it difficult to communicate directly with one another in the interests of the child with whom they are all concerned. They are made for periods of six months.

It is hoped that, through the skilled intervention of a probation officer or social worker, the adults and/or children involved in situations of emotional difficulty will be helped to put feelings of hurt or bitterness aside in the interests of children.

Does the Mother always Get the Children?

Family lawyers are frequently asked this question when there is a dispute between parents about where children should live. Fathers often believe that they are at a disadvantage when it comes to a court making this kind of decision.

The answer is that parents start off, so far as the law is concerned, on equal terms. There is no particular magic in being a mother. Every child is an individual, with his or her own individual set of characteristics and circumstances. The court will do its utmost to ensure that, for the particular child in any case, the decision made will be in that child's best interests.

That means taking account of all the circumstances. One circumstance which cannot be ignored is that, in most cases, it is often thought that a baby or a very young child will be more adequately cared for by a mother than a father.

Again, this is not true of all babies or very young children. Many modern fathers are equally capable of caring for their children from babyhood. Some mothers do not provide the best care. Each case will be decided after careful investigation of all the circumstances including, of course, the ascertainable wishes and feelings of the child, if he or she is old enough to understand what is going on.

As children grow older, the undeniable tilt of the scales in the mother's favour becomes less significant. But another factor which will be taken into account, if it exists, is that the mother may be available on a full-time basis to care for the children while the father has a full-time job.

Not every full-time mother succeeds in obtaining a residence order where the father has a full-time job. Again, each case depends on the circumstances.

The guiding principle for the court will always be to discover what will be in the best interests of the child.

Is there a New Bias towards Fathers?

A fairly recent development has been the publicity given in the media to cases where fathers have been given residence orders in circumstances where it is the mother who has, in fact, been the breadwinner, perhaps because of better job qualifications, while the father has remained at home caring for young children and acting as 'househusband'.

These cases do not, as is often wrongly asserted, demonstrate any change in the approach of the courts to disputes about with which parent a child should live. They are merely examples of the court applying the test of what is in the best interests of the children concerned.

Career women may well reflect that they could be shooting themselves in the foot in these days of equality and the 'new man'. But it is the parent who represents the significant caring figure on a day to day basis in the child's life who is the most likely to obtain a residence order, regardless of whether that parent happens to be Mummy or Daddy.

Useful Addresses

The National Council for One Parent Families
255 Kentish Town Road
London NW5 2LX
Telephone: 0171 267 1361

The Child Poverty Action Group
94 White Lion Street
London N1 9PF
Telephone: 0171 837 7979

Families Need Fathers (helps non-residential parents and their
    children)
134 Curtin Road
London EC2A 3AR
Telephone: 0171 6135060

Children – North East
1a Claremont Street
Newcastle Upon Tyne NE2 4AH
Telephone: 0191 232 3741

Parent Network (support and education groups for parents)
Winchester House
11 Cranmer Road
London SW9 6EJ
Telephone: 0171 485 8535

Network of Acess and Child Contact Centres (NACCC)
Minerva House
Spaniel Row
Nottingham NG1 6EP
Telephone: 0115 948 4557

CHAPTER SEVEN

HOW THE LAW CAN HELP YOU TO REACH AN AGREEMENT

Ideally, when the relationship of parents breaks down the parents themselves should be able to discuss the future of their children together. Putting their own feelings aside, they should concentrate on the simple truth that, whereas relationships between parents may not necessarily endure, parenthood is for life.

Effects of Parental Separation on Children

Recent research carried out on behalf of the Joseph Rowntree Foundation, concluded that children of separated families have a higher probability of:

(a) being in poverty and poor housing;

(b) being poorer when they are adults;

(c) behavioural problems;

(d) performing less well in school;

(e) needing medical treatment;

(f) leaving school/home when young;

(g) becoming sexually active, pregnant or a parent at an early age;

(h) depressive symptoms, high levels of smoking and drinking and drug use during adolescence and adulthood.

Among the factors affecting the outcome of separation of their parents on children were that:

(a) family conflict before, during and after separation can contribute to behavioural problems in children;

(b) a parent's ability to recover from the distress of separation can contribute to behavioural problems in the children;

(c) multiple changes in family structure increase the probability of poor outcomes for children;

(d) quality contact with the non-resident parent can improve outcomes.

The researchers concluded that support for parents to help them deal with the distress of separation is needed so that they, in turn, are better able to help their children. They felt that information needs to be given to parents to help them understand that separation does not necessarily lead to adverse effects, but that factors such as conflict between the parents can be damaging for the children. They believe that ongoing contact by the non-residential parent should be supported, except where protection from violence or abuse is necessary, and they point out that support at times of forming step-families may be as important as support following separation.

Not very surprisingly, it is the unanimous view of the experts who have conducted these investigations that the children who best survive the breakdown of the parents' relationship are those whose parents are able to communicate with each other without recrimination and bitterness. Separating or separated parents who can talk to one another about matters concerning their children give the children reassurance that they are still loved and important and will continue to be so.

This is why there has been such an increasing emphasis on trying to help partners to face their problems and seek solutions to them together rather than battling out their differences through the courts. The process is known as conciliation. The new divorce law, which has not yet come into effect, has been set out in detail in Chapter 4. The provision of conciliation opportunities is to be central to the operation of the new procedure. In the meantime, the courts are continuing to offer conciliation appointments where parents are in dispute about future plans for their children.

What is Conciliation?

The dictionary definition of the verb 'to conciliate' is 'to win over
from anger or hostility, to win goodwill'. Many people confuse conciliation with 'reconciliation', and mistakenly believe that a conciliation appointment will mean that attempts will be made to persuade
them against separation.

Conciliation is a process of attempting to pour oil on troubled
waters. In any dispute a conciliator listens to what each side has to
say and then attempts to find some common ground or to negotiate
between the disputants to reach an agreement with which both will
be reasonably content. There is no attempt, or indeed intent, to arrive at a 'kiss and make up' situation.

The Appointment

Conciliation appointments were introduced into the courts as a way
of trying to avoid the bitterness and recrimination which frequently
arose between warring parents in the course of court proceedings. It
has been found to be very helpful to most parents to be given an
opportunity to explore the possibilities of agreement on mutual ground
with the assistance of a skilled mediator.

It had been the experience of the courts that, when evidence of
one parent's complaints against the other had been written down in
the form of affidavits or statements for the court, the level of bitterness was bound to escalate. It was therefore decided that a conciliation process at court should be introduced, to take place before any
written evidence had been filed or seen by either parent.

The advantages of the conciliation appointment are:

(a) it gives the parents a chance to reach agreement, with the assistance of skilled help and before written allegations made by one
against the other exacerbate an already difficult situation;

(b) if successful, it results in great savings in time and expense.

Will there always be a Conciliation Appointment?

It is usual for the court to fix a conciliation appointment where there is a dispute about a child between the child's parents. However, a conciliation appointment is not always fixed in applications about children. If the court considers that the level of bitterness between the parents is such that there is no realistic possibility of conciliation being successful, it may not fix the appointment.

What happens at the Appointment?

Once the application about the child has been filed with the court, whether by a solicitor acting for a parent, or by a parent himself or herself, the date and time fixed for the conciliation appointment will be given to both parents. The appointment will be with a district judge of the court where the application has been made. The district judge will take the appointment, together with a court welfare officer.

Who should attend the Appointment?

Each of the parents should attend the appointment, together with legal advisers if any. The children should also be brought to the appointment, if they are over nine years of age; sometimes even younger children attend.

Do not be worried by this appointment as usually the atmosphere is as relaxed and informal as possible. When the case is called on, the parents, with their legal advisers if they are legally represented, will go into the court. Normally, in the court of a district judge, everyone sits around a long table. The district judge will be at the top of the table, with the court welfare officer. The parents and legal advisers sit on either side of the table.

The district judge will introduce the welfare officer to the parents. If the parent making the application is legally represented, the barrister or solicitor representing him or her will briefly tell the district judge about the application. The judge will be informed about the dates of birth of the children concerned, when and in what circumstances the parents separated, and about the application itself. The facts should be stated neutrally, since the whole aim of the appointment is, as far as humanly possible, to avoid an atmosphere where one parent scores points against the other. The barrister or solicitor representing the other parent will then be given an opportunity to define the area of disagreement, and should again be taking care to be as non-controversial as possible.

If one or both parents are in person, unrepresented by a barrister or solicitor, the district judge may ask a few direct questions in order to clarify the areas of dispute.

Any children who are attending the conciliation appointment will be asked to wait outside the court while these preliminary introductions are going on.

The Conciliation Process

Everyone then comes out of the court, hopefully into some reasonably comfortable area. In the Principal Registry of the Family Division, in London, conciliation appointments take place in a suite of rooms which have been furnished with comfortable chairs and equipped with a machine which dispenses hot and cold drinks, crisps, biscuits and confectionery. This helps to promote a relaxed and friendly atmosphere, which is vitally important to the whole idea of conciliation.

Unfortunately, conditions in other courts around the country vary enormously, with the worst – all too frequent – situation being that the parents, the children and their legal advisers all sit on hard benches ranged along the walls of some dreary court corridor, where there are no refreshment facilities and an atmosphere calculated to make everyone concerned feel thoroughly miserable. Not really conducive to the conciliation process!

The court welfare officer decides how to handle the conciliation process. This will almost certainly involve, in no particular order, discussing the dispute:

(a) with the parents together without the children;

(b) with each of the parents on their own;

(c) with the children, sometimes together and sometimes singly, depending on the circumstances of the case;

(d) with the parents and children all together.

The whole process can be very short, or it might take as long as a day. The idea is for the welfare officer first to identify the precise areas of dispute between the parents. He or she then attempts to find any areas where there may be agreement. From that point, attempts will be made to negotiate a full agreement on the points disputed, helping the parents to bear in mind that it is unlikely that one or the other will achieve exactly what he or she wants, and that it is infinitely better to settle matters between themselves than to have a solution imposed by the court, which may not be acceptable to either of them.

The attendance of the children, if they are old enough, is of vital importance. It often happens that a child is too torn between loyalties to be able to tell one or both parents what his or her view of the dispute might be. The welfare officer will be skilled in relating to children and will frequently be able to communicate the child's wishes and feelings about the dispute to both parents, sometimes with the result that any disagreements can be resolved there and then.

What is the point of having Lawyers there?

If one or both parents is legally represented, a barrister or solicitor will attend the conciliation appointment with that parent. Unusually for court appointments, the lawyer will be – or ought to be – keeping a low profile. However, if a settlement of the dispute is being negotiated the parents might wish to consult their legal advisers, who will be able to assist with the drafting of a consent order to be made by the court should any agreement be reached.

If the conciliation appointment has been successful and the parents have reached agreement, everyone goes back into the court before the judge, who makes the order which has been agreed. In some cases, agreement is such that the judge might decide that it is preferable to make no order at all, since the parents, after discussion with the welfare officer, have decided to exercise their own parental responsibility for making decisions about their children without the necessity for a court order.

On the other hand, if the conciliation has not been successful, everyone goes back into court, and the judge gives directions for how the case will continue.

Where no agreement has been reached, the judge will almost certainly order the preparation of a court welfare officer's report. directed to the question in dispute. However, the welfare officer who makes the report will not be the one who has been involved in the conciliation appointment. This is to ensure that nothing said by anyone in the course of a conciliation appointment can affect the evidence given to the court when the case comes to be heard.

Confidentiality

Do be assured that nothing which is said by anyone in the course of a conciliation appointment can be repeated in any subsequent hearing of the matter by the court, whether in writing in a statement filed with the court or in oral evidence. The legal expression for this is that the discussions which take place during conciliation are 'privileged'.

CASE STUDY

Jeremy has applied for contact with his daughter Angela, who is six years old. Angela's mother, Joan, is opposed to Jeremy having any contact with her. Jeremy and Joan separated when Angela was two years old and Angela has not seen her father since then. Joan says that Angela has forgotten her father. Joan has a new husband, Peter, who has taken over the role of father in Angela's life.

A conciliation appointment is arranged. Jeremy and Joan attend the appointment. In the course of discussions with the court welfare officer, Joan admits in Jeremy's presence that the principal reason for her opposition to the reintroduction of Jeremy into Angela's life is Peter's jealousy of Jeremy.

The conciliation appointment is not successful. Jeremy's application for contact will have to be heard by a judge, and the judge gives directions for signed statements to be filed by Jeremy and Joan, setting out their respective positions. It appears to Jeremy that the fact that Peter is unreasonably jealous of him is not a good reason for denying him contact with Angela.

In his signed statement, or in his oral evidence to the court when his application is heard, can Jeremy refer to Joan's admission that her principal reason for refusing to agree to his having contact with Angela is that Peter is jealous of Jeremy?

The answer must be no. What Joan told the court welfare officer in Jeremy's presence during the conciliation process is privileged. Jeremy may not refer to it in his statement or in his oral evidence.

The Exception to the Rule of Confidentiality

There is one exception to the privilege which is given to anything which is said in the course of a conciliation appointment. The exception is when anything is said which indicates that a child might be at serious risk.

For example, suppose during the conciliation discussions, Joan had admitted to the court welfare officer that, on occasions when she had lost her temper with Angela, she had been slapping her much too hard, to the extent that she had twice bruised the little girl so badly that she had kept her away from school so that the bruising would not be noticed. The privilege attached to the conciliation process would be overridden by the primary duty to have regard to the best interests of Angela, and her mother's disclosure could be reported by the court welfare officer to the social services department for the area where Joan and Angela were living.

There have been attempts to persuade the court that discussions which took place in the course of conciliation or mediation were not strictly privileged, so that things said by one or other person or by the conciliator might be disclosed if they were at all relevant to the case.

However, the Court of Appeal made the position clear in a recent case, when it was stated that evidence could not be given of statements made by people in the course of conciliation sessions 'save in the very unusual case where a statement is made clearly indicating that the maker has in the past caused or is likely in the future to cause serious harm to the well being of a child'.

The Reasons for Confidentiality

This confidentiality demonstrates the importance which the courts attach to encouraging people who are caught up in family disputes to try to resolve them with skilled help rather than taking them to a full-scale court battle. People will be less worried about possible repercussions if they can be assured that what they say in the process of mediation or conciliation will remain completely confidential. With the reduction in eligibility for legal aid, the mediation process is likely to seem an infinitely more attractive – because it is a much less expensive – way of resolving conflicts than slugging them out in court.

This can only be to the ultimate advantage of parents and, more importantly, to the advantage of the unfortunate children at the centre of parental quarrels.

CHAPTER EIGHT

THE COURT WELFARE REPORT

If you are involved in a case concerning your child, the court may ask for a welfare report. This is nothing to be concerned about; it is simply used to assist the court to reach a decision. The court will direct that the report should deal with a specific question or questions, and any report prepared will normally be limited to those questions. However, it occasionally happens that a report will deal with wider matters concerning the child and the various people involved, rather than limiting itself strictly to the areas indicated by the court.

The purpose of welfare reports is to assist the court by giving a fuller picture of the child's situation and all the factors relevant to any decision the court is being asked to make. For example, if there is a dispute about with which parent a child should live, the welfare officer will visit the child in both homes. If there is a dispute about contact the welfare officer may decide to observe the child's reaction to the parent who wants contact. By ordering a welfare report, the court is not handing over the task of making the decision to a welfare officer. The decision is for the court alone.

However, it is true to say that the court will almost always pay a great deal of attention to any recommendation made in a welfare report. Indeed, if a judge does not make an order in accordance with a recommendation by a court welfare officer, he must state his reasons for not doing so.

Not every welfare report contains recommendations about the decisions which the court is being asked to make. Some welfare reports simply set out the information which the officer has been able to obtain, possibly together with some impressions of the various people interviewed in the course of the investigations, but making no firm recommendation on what should be the order made, leaving it to the court to make the final decision.

The Form of the Report

Welfare reports may be made in writing or orally. If the matter is not one of urgency, it is usual for the court to request a written report. One of the reasons for this is in order to give the parties involved in the court proceedings some notice of what the welfare officer will be saying or recommending. This means that consideration can be given to questions which might be asked of the officer who prepared the report.

Oral Reports by Court Welfare Officers

However, if the matter is very urgent, or if for some other reason the court considers it preferable, the report may be requested on the basis that the reporting officer will give only an oral report.

CASE STUDY

Matthew, who is ten years old, is living with his mother Anne and her new husband James, as a result of the court deciding that Matthew should live with his mother. Sam, Matthew's father, has been allowed to have Matthew staying with him for alternate weekends.

Sam goes to court one Monday morning. He asks the judge to discharge the existing residence order in Anne's favour and to make an order that Matthew should live with him. He says that when the child had been due to return to his mother on the previous evening he had broken down in tears and had begged Sam to let him stay with him. Sam says that Matthew was so distressed that he was unable to persuade him to go back. Matthew had told him that he hated James, and that James was punishing him excessively and unfairly by locking him in a dark cupboard for hours on end.

The judge is faced with an extremely difficult situation. Sam has informed Anne of his application and she too has come to court to ask for an order that Matthew should be returned to her immediately. She categorically denies that James has been punishing Matthew by locking him in an unlit cupboard. She says that Sam is probably making all this up because he wants Mathew to live with him.

It is in this kind of case that a judge might well ask a

welfare officer to talk to Mathew and report back on an oral basis, rather than waiting for a written report, which might very well take weeks or months to prepare. It is obviously an urgent matter. Judges are always reluctant to change existing orders without good reason. They are even more reluctant to do so on an emergency basis, preferring to wait until all possible evidence, including a welfare report if appropriate, is before the court.

On the other hand, if Sam is accurately reporting what has been said by Matthew, there is clearly cause for concern about whether he should return to his mother.

In such an urgent situation, where a judge has asked a welfare officer for an oral report, the period of time given for the preparation of the report might be a few days, or even a few hours. It is actually possible for a court welfare officer to be requested to see both parents and the child in the court building so as to be able to report back immediately.

The welfare officer would undoubtedly speak to Sam and Anne before attempting to talk to Mathew. He or she would then expect to be introduced to Matthew, by both parents if possible.

Fortunately, the vast majority of court welfare officers are highly skilled and very sensitive in their approach to children. For example, it is extremely unlikely that the welfare officer would ask Matthew straight away whether he has any problems with his stepfather; he or she would have to approach the matter as seems best at the time. It would be usual for the officer to sit down somewhere quietly with the child, hopefully in a room comfortably furnished for such meetings, and simply have a general chat with him.

Matthew might be asked about his school, what subjects he likes best, which games he prefers. The welfare officer might then ask him about his friends, both school friends and those he plays with when he is at home. Gradually, and in a natural way, the welfare officer would take time to encourage Matthew to feel relaxed. Only when Matthew's confidence had been gained would the welfare officer approach the question of what was troubling Matthew, possibly by way of an enquiry about with which parent he was living and how often he saw the other parent.

In this way, the discussion could eventually get to a point where the welfare officer could discuss Matthew's reluctance to return home. It is possible that Mathew has indeed

good cause to complain about his stepfather's treatment of
him. On the other hand, it is not unknown for a parent with
whom the child does not live to 'manufacture' complaints,
for example by encouraging a child to give a wildly exagger-
ated account of perfectly normal discipline.

When the officer feels ready to make a report in a case
like Matthew's, the parents return to the court and the welfare officer reports the discussion with Matthew to the judge.
The judge will then give each of the parents, or their legal
representatives, an opportunity to put questions to the officer and to make any submissions as to what the decision
about Matthew should be. The judge then makes a decision
based upon all the evidence which he has read and heard.

Written Reports

Matthew's case was one of emergency. Most reports made by court
welfare officers are prepared in writing and at a much more leisurely
pace. Conciliation appointments have already been discussed in
Chapter 7, however, there are cases where disputes between parents
can only be resolved by a court hearing. In these cases, a court welfare officer will be asked to investigate the dispute and provide a full
written report. A different welfare officer will be appointed so that
anything said during conciliation remains confidential.

How Long will it Take?

One of the stated aims of the Children Act was the avoidance of
delay in deciding questions relating to children. Judges hearing children's cases are always very keen to have them decided as quickly as
possible in order to avoid causing unnecessary stress to parents and,
more importantly, to children.

In an ideal world this would mean that delays were kept to a
minimum in children cases. Unfortunately, although everyone concerned is committed to moving things along as quickly as possible,
financial constraints mean that families frequently have to wait for
periods of several months before a case can be heard. The time taken
to prepare welfare reports varies from court to court; a period of
three to four months is not at all unusual. Some courts will fix a
hearing date before the welfare report has been made available, other

courts will not fix a date until the report has actually been filed.

If the court waits until the welfare report has actually been filed, there may well be a further delay of several months before a hearing date can be given. This means that it is not at all uncommon for cases to take six months, and sometimes even up to and more than a year, to come before the court to be decided.

When one looks at this in human terms, it can result in enormous frustration and even downright misery for the parents and children concerned.

CASE STUDY

David and Cheryl have become unhappy in their marriage and have decided to divorce. They have four children, Donna who is thirteen years old, Alan who is ten years old, Susannah who is six years old and Charlie who is five years old. David and Cheryl have been quite unable to agree with whom the children should live after they separate. Each has applied to the court asking for the children to live with him or her.

There has been a conciliation appointment, attended by the children as well as by David and Cheryl. The court welfare officer was unable to help he parents to reach agreement. A welfare report, which will be prepared by a different officer, has been ordered.

David and Cheryl occupy a semi-detached house which they are buying with a mortgage in their joint names. It is accepted that whoever has the children will continue to live in the home. The other parent will leave.

Neither David nor Cheryl is prepared to leave until the court decides which of them is to have the children. The house has only three bedrooms, the third of which is very small. Since David moved out of their bedroom, Cheryl has been sharing the main bedroom with Susannah. Alan and Charlie share the second bedroom and Donna has the very small bedroom. David has a put-u-up bed in the living-room.

David and Cheryl try to behave in a normal way for he sake of the children. But the tensions are quite obvious and have their effects upon the children. Cheryl does not cook meals for David and she does no washing or ironing for him. She and David barely speak to one another. The whole atmosphere in the home is highly stressful. Donna's school work is suffering, Alan has become cheeky and is getting out of control, Susannah is weepy and clingy and Charlie has started bed-wetting, having been dry at night since he was two.

The situation of David and Cheryl and their children is a distressingly common one. Neither parent will agree to leave the home until the matter has been decided by the court, for fear that the other parent would gain the advantage of the 'status quo' argument.

'Status quo' is an expression which is popular with lawyers involved in family cases, particularly where there are disputes about residence. Roughly translated, it means the situation as it exists. Lawyers arguing a case will place great emphasis on the benefits to a child of not interfering with the status quo – the situation to which the child is accustomed.

It cannot be denied that court welfare officers and judges are reluctant to interfere with the status quo, where it appears to be working reasonably well, in case such interference would bring about a worse situation. It follows that if you are the parent who is actually caring for a child when a dispute about residence comes to court, you have an undoubted advantage.

It is for this reason that a family lawyer would be unable to advise either David or Cheryl to leave the home pending a resolution of the dispute about who is to be the day to day carer for the children. The parent who left would immediately be giving the other the advantage.

Unfortunately far too many families are forced to live in a stressful situation such as that experienced by David and Cheryl. Unless more resources can be directed towards the provision of an increased number of court welfare officers, court buildings and judges there seems little hope that such families can be spared prolonged unhappiness.

The Preparation of the Report

Once a written report has been ordered by the court, the welfare officer has the duty to investigate all those matters to which the court directs the officer's attention. The reporting officer might be requested to examine the more general question of time spent with each parent, or something more specific, such as a choice of school for a child.

Welfare reports can be ordered in any case concerning a child. If a grandparent or other interested adult should be given permission to make an application with regard to a child, a report can be ordered by the court just as in disputes between parents.

The welfare officer will read any documentation available on the court file. Sometimes there will be statements by the parents, and other witnesses, if these have been ordered by the court. In other cases the court might direct that no statements should be filed until all parties have had a chance to read the report. Often a statement will contain things which will anger one party, for this reason the court will often delay asking for statements, in order to keep the heat out of the situation for as long as possible while attempts are being made to bring the parties to agreement by means of conciliation.

Court welfare officers are, of course, individuals. Each one approaches the task of preparing a report in his or her individual way, but there are certain guidelines which the courts have given them to follow.

CASE STUDY

Delia and Kevin have a six year old son, Colin. Delia and Kevin are living apart. Each has applied to the court for Colin to live with them. There was a conciliation appointment but it did not result in an agreement about where Colin should live. The court has ordered a welfare report, to be directed to the question of whether it will be in Colin's best interests to live with his mother or his father.

Delia lives in the home she originally shared with Kevin, a two-bedroom flat. No one else lives there. Kevin has moved to another two-bedroom flat, so the accommodation which could be offered to the child by each parent is approximately the same.

The court welfare officer interviews Delia, alone and with Colin. Both interviews take place in Delia's flat. The court welfare officer interviews Kevin, alone and with Colin. Both these interviews take place at the offices of social services for the area.

The court welfare officer then files his report. The report ends with a firm recommendation that Delia's application should be granted and Kevin's rejected.

There may well be many good reasons for the recommendation made by the court welfare officer that Colin should live with his mother rather than with his father, but Kevin

would have a legitimate reason to challenge the report and
its recommendation. Because the Court of Appeal has made
it clear that, when a report is ordered relating to the question of with which parent a child is to live, the child should
be observed by the court welfare officer with each of the
parents in his or her home environment.

A welfare officer who does not carry out that duty to see the child in
both homes runs the risk that any recommendations given will be
viewed as of little help in the decision making process for the judge.

Indeed, in a residence dispute where a welfare officer has not
taken the trouble to visit the child in both homes, the court might
well order a further report to be made by the officer after visits to
each home have been carried out.

The Child's Wishes and Feelings

One of the most important considerations for the court in any question relating to a child is what may be the wishes and feelings of that
child. As has already been pointed out, the older the child, the more
he or she can understand and appreciate what the dispute is about,
the more regard the court will pay to what he/she wants.

In most cases about children which have to be decided by the
court, the person who will explore the child's wishes and feelings
and communicate them to the court will be the welfare officer.

It has to be remembered that when arguments about children get
as far as a court hearing, adult emotions and even tempers are likely
to be running at a high level. For example, it would be most unusual
for any parent to continue a battle about where children should live
without being absolutely convinced in his or her own mind that the
children's wishes and feelings were identical with his or hers.

The temptation for a parent involved in such a dispute to encourage the child to tell the court welfare officer what that parent wants
the officer to hear, can be too great in some cases. This leads to the
desperately sad situation where a child can be subjected to the most
unbearable emotional pressure by one or both parents. The parent
becomes so wrapped up in determination to 'win' that the effects of
the emotional temperature on the child are completely disregarded.

There are cases where parents simply never give up on the battle, even after a court decision has been made. Some parents will go on subjecting their children to pressure, just to get back at the other parent. The unfortunate children of such parents often bear the emotional scars into their adult lives.

Questioning the Court Welfare Officer

The report of the court welfare officer will normally be filed some time before the hearing date, and copies will be sent to all concerned. At this stage, as at all stages, the parents can, and often do, make their own decision without the need for a court hearing. But if there has to be a hearing the judge will give each of the parties or their legal representative yourself, if any, an opportunity to question the court welfare officer. If you are representing yourself and you wish to ask a welfare officer questions about the report, you must ask the court to ensure that the officer will be available on the day of the hearing.

If you yourself are asking the questions, it is a good idea to make a list of them before coming to court. Always ask the questions as politely as you can. The judge will never be impressed by rudeness to the court welfare officer, and you can be quite sure that the judge will listen with close attention to any questions you may ask, and to the replies given, before coming to a decision.

After the Hearing

Some court welfare officers will offer to make themselves available to the parties to give advice and assistance on an informal basis after the hearing. This can often be very helpful in smoothing initial difficulties.

CHAPTER NINE

CHILD SUPPORT

What is Child Support Maintenance?

Child support maintenance is an amount of money which a non-resident parent pays regularly as a contribution to the financial support of his or her child.

Until April 1993, when the parents of a child had separated the usual means of obtaining a financial contribution towards the maintenance of the child was by way of a court order. There were cases, of course, where the parents were able to agree what the contribution should be and then there would be no need for an order of the court.

You will probably have seen many news reports about absent fathers being chased for maintenance. This has come about due to the Child Support Act which came into force in 1993, and which completely changed the approach to child maintenance. With hindsight it can be seen that the effect of the change, which set up the Child Support Agency for the assessment and collection of child maintenance, has been far from what had been hoped.

Background

The objectives behind the child support legislation were understandable. Firstly, it formed part of an overall determination by the government to emphasise that parents were responsible for their own children. In 1989, the Children Act had started the process of underlining the fact that being a parent carries responsibilities rather than rights. In 1991, the Criminal Justice Act had extended the powers of the court to impose penalties on those with parental responsibility for delinquent children. The Child Support Act was the third plank in the government's programme.

Financial considerations were of considerable significance. There had been growing concern about the level of payments being ordered by courts and the resultant burden on the state when social security payments had to make up the difference between the maintenance ordered and income support rates.

Throughout the 1980s, there had been attempts made to persuade courts to make orders in line with current income support rates, but these had largely been unsuccessful. In 1990, the average maintenance being ordered for a child, of any age up to eighteen, was £18 per week. In that year, the National Foster Care Association was recommending payments of £34.02 per week for a child under the age of five.

Increasing numbers of parents were separating, and the consequently increased burden upon the taxpayer was becoming insupportable. Having failed to get the courts to raise the level of orders being made, the government decided to set up the Child Support Agency as a completely separate entity, which would be under governmental control.

Unfortunately, it soon became clear that there are aspects of the child support scheme which are causing considerable public disquiet. At first it was hoped that most of the difficulties were simply teething problems which could be remedied by fine tuning although it became obvious that the problems were deep-seated.

'Caring' and 'Absent'?

Probably one of the most tactless aspects of the child support scheme was in its use of terminology. It ought to have been foreseeable that to describe parents as either 'caring' or 'absent' was going to cause trouble. This should have been particularly obvious in the context of the Children Act which had just deliberately enacted the words 'residence' and 'contact' in place of the emotive 'custody' and 'access'.

Not every parent who does not have day to day care of his or her child is in that position from choice. Moreover, many parents who do not care for their children on a day to day basis are still concerned, loving parents, who wish to play as full a part in the lives of the children as possible.

Not surprisingly, such parents found being categorised as 'absent' hurtful, particularly when it was contrasted with 'caring'. Thankfully, the government has appreciated the sensitivity of this aspect and some changes have been introduced by the government to take account of these problems.

The Formula

The financial contribution which must be made by the absent parent for the maintenance of his or her child is calculated by means of a formula. The formula at present is fairly rigid and is extremely difficult to understand.

The rigidity of the formula was intended to ensure that every absent parent had his or her contribution worked out in accordance with a strict mathematical calculation which was applied in every case. This is to be contrasted with the somewhat haphazard situation in operation before the child support legislation, which meant that two judges sitting in the same court in different cases might make two completely different maintenance orders given the same figures to work on. Unfortunately, experience has shown that assessments by the agency are at least as likely to result in unfairness.

There have been criticisms that the formula does not make allowance for some of the outgoings of the absent parent, to the point where he or she can be reduced to an income below that of income support by its operation. Payment of instalments in relation to certain debts is not taken into account, for example.

If the absent parent lives at some distance from the children, cost of travel to and from contact visits is not taken into account. This is another matter which has caused considerable concern.

Second wives bitterly resent the levels of contribution being sought by the Child Support Agency for the children of their husbands' first marriages, particularly where the first wife has remarried and lives in comfortable financial circumstances with her new husband.

Natural Fathers

The parents liable to maintain a child under the child support legislation are the child's natural parents. Before the Child Support Act came into force, a father would have been liable for any child he had treated as a child of the family during the marriage. This change in the law has had some unforeseen consequences.

CASE STUDY

When Ben met Sherrie she had a baby, Rachel, who was a few months old. Ben and Sherrie married and Ben always treated Rachel as his own child. Ben and Sherrie later had two more children, Marcel and Barnabas. If Ben and Sherrie separated, Ben would be liable to maintain Marcel and Barnabas under child support law but not Rachel, even though he always treated Rachel in exactly the same way as his own children. This would probably leave Rachel, if now a teenager, feeling hurt and bewildered that there should be a difference between her and her brothers, when she has always looked on Ben as her own father too.

Sherrie is on income support. The child support officer asks her to name Rachel's father so that he can be traced and made to pay maintenance for Rachel.

Naming the Father

It is a requirement of the child support legislation that a mother on income support should identify the natural father of her child. If she refuses to do so, she can be penalised by a reduction in the amount of benefit she is paid, unless she can demonstrate that to identify the father would put her or any child living with her at risk.

This provision has the unfortunate practical result that a father who has used violence against the mother or a child in the past will be able to evade responsibility for child support. In the circumstances, it is hardly surprising if responsible and law-abiding fathers believe that the operation of the child support legislation is producing an unfair result.

As only the natural father of a child is liable for maintenance under the operation of the child support law, it is predicted that some fathers will seek to deny paternity in order to escape liability. Under the old law, if a child had been accepted as a child of the family by the father, he would be liable to maintain that child when his marriage broke down. It is more than possible that many fathers who suspected that a child was not theirs during a marriage may now wish to put that suspicion to the test.

Unfortunately, applications made in such circumstances may well have serious repercussions so far as the unfortunate child is concerned, not to mention the effect upon the relationship between the divorced parents.

Applying for Child Support Maintenance

Who can apply for Child Maintenance?

The Agency normally only deals with cases where both parents live in Great Britain or Northern Ireland. Subject to that you can apply if:

(a) you are a parent of a child or children who are living with you while the other parent lives somewhere else, unless you have a court maintenance order or written maintenance agreement made before 5 April 1993;

(b) children, who are not your own, live with you while their parent or parents live somewhere else;

(c) if you are a parent not living with your child, or children, and you wish to have an assessment carried out to show the amount of maintenance you ought to pay.

When you must apply

If you are a parent with care of a child or children and you or your current partner gets one of the following benefits you may be required to apply for child maintenance assessment:

(a) income support; or

(b) family credit; or

(c) disability working allowance; or

(d) income-based job seeker's allowance.

If you are so required, then you must authorise the Agency to follow up getting maintenance from the other parent.

As maintained above, if you believe that giving the Agency authority to get maintenance from the other parent will lead to harm or undue distress for you or any child living with you, whether or not that child is the child of the other parent, you may ask the Agency to agree that you do not have to give them this authority. Staff from the Agency will want to discuss any such request with you.

What happens if a Child spends time with both Parents?

It your child spends part of the time with you and part of the time with the other parent, the child support maintenance will be shared, provided that the child spends an average of two nights a week, at least 104 nights a year, with the absent parent.

How will the Agency Contact absent Parents?

If you are the parent with care you will be asked to give information about the absent parent, for example his or her name and address and date of birth. If you do not know the address, the Agency will try to find it by, for example, checking national insurance and inland revenue records. The Agency will not give the address of one parent to the other without the agreement of both parents.

What happens if the absent Parent refuses to give information?

If the absent parent refuses to complete the form which is sent requesting details of his or her income and outgoings the Agency can make an interim assessment, which will usually be higher than the assessment which would be made with full information about the absent parent's means. The absent parent will then be compelled to pay at the interim assessment rate until he or she provides sufficient information for a full assessment to be made.

How does an absent Parent pay?

If you are an absent parent you can pay directly to the parent with care by cheque, standing order or postal order. Alternatively, you can make the payments though the Child Support Agency by direct debit, post office transcash, or through a bank to the Agency's account. The payments can be made weekly, monthly, or at some other agreed intervals. If the absent parent does not make the payments assessed, and does not have an acceptable reason for failing to do so, the Agency can have the payments deducted from the parent's wages or salary at source. However, if an absent parent's financial circumstances change, he or she can apply for a new assessment to be made. If you are an absent parent who is on income support and you an over eighteen, fit to work and with no dependent children living with you, you may be required to contribute a minimum sum, the amount of which is changed from time to time, weekly towards the maintenance of your children.

How is the Maintenance worked out?

The Agency takes into account:

(a) the day to day cost of maintaining a child;

(b) the income of both parents after allowing for tax, national insurance and basic expenses, rent or mortgage costs for example;

(c) any other children either parent may have.

An absent parent should not have to pay more than 30 per cent of his or her net income in maintenance. If the paying parent is in arrears with payments, he or she will not normally be expected to pay more than 33 per cent of net income, unless he or she has failed to respond promptly or fully to a request for information.

If the parent with children living with him or her has a new partner, the new partner will not be expected to pay anything towards the child support maintenance of any child not his or her natural child. Equally, a new partner of a paying parent will not be expected to make any contribution to the maintenance of the children for whom that parent is paying.

Collection Service

The Child Support Agency offers a collection service in addition to the assessment and review service. If asked to do so, it will collect the payments from the absent parent and pass them on to the parent with care. If the absent parent falls behind with the payments, the Agency will consider taking action to enforce them.

The Future for Child Support

It cannot be said that the Child Support Agency has successfully operated the scheme over the years since the system came into force. Collection and enforcement of payments, the most important work of the agency has been taking up only 10 per cent of the time of agency staff, with the overwhelming 90 per cent of the time being taken up by assessment and reassessment. One of the root causes of this problem is undoubtedly the fantastically complex method of assessment, based as it is on a mathematical formula which is so obscure that only people with maths to A-level standard seem to be able to understand it!

There has been enormous dissatisfaction on all sides. Parents with children residing with them complain that assessments are too low and/or that the parent who should be making the payments refuses to do so and gets away with it. Non-resident parents complain that the assessments are far too high. Taxpayers get the feeling that enormous sums of public money are being wasted to bolster up a system which is inefficient, penalises the poorest and seems to enable many high-earning, absent parents to escape making appropriate payments for the maintenance of their children. In July 1998, figures were disclosed which revealed that one-third of receipts from non-resident parents and almost four out of five maintenance balances for full assessments were for the wrong amount!

Many family lawyers believe that the old system, when the courts assessed the amount of maintenance which should be paid for children taking into account all the circumstances of the parents, was more efficient, cheaper and fairer. However, the government is committed to the idea of what are basically non-discretionary payments administered by an agency.

The government has admitted, however, that the present system operates unfairly and inefficiently and is not enforced with sufficient firmness. Proposals to reform it were published in July 1998, with the objective of setting a simpler assessment formula, so that parents could understand and, hopefully, accept it. Unfortunately, it is not anticipated that this new system will come into operation until the year 2001!

It is good to note, at least, that the term 'absent parent' which was criticised in the earlier edition of this book, is to be replaced by 'non-resident parent'.

One of the most important features of the proposed changes is that, in future, liability to maintain children should be based on a simple percentage of the non-resident parent's net income, 15 per cent for one child, 20 per cent for two and 25 per cent for three or more.

'Shared care' at present means that the child must spend a minimum of 104 nights a year with the non-resident parent; it is proposed that this should be reduced to 52 nights a year.

The Poorest Families

Three-quarters of parents with care are receiving income support. In order to help these families, their benefits will not be reduced pound for pound by any child maintenance paid as at present, and they will be allowed to keep the first £10 before the payments are reduced.

But the penalties imposed on parents with care of their children who refuse to co-operate with the Agency can only result in hardship for the children in the poorest families during the periods in which benefit income is cut. The Child Poverty Action Group is concerned that no comment has been made by the government on this issue; indeed there has been an indication that the government would wish to reduce the time taken to impose the penalty.

Useful Information

Child Support Agency, Enquiry Line:
Telephone: 0345 133 133 (9 am – 6pm. Weekdays; calls charged on local rate).

For Parents Who Live Apart – leaflet issued by DSS explaining child support. It is obtainable in post offices, local benefit offices, County Court offices, Citizens Advice Bureaux, etc.

The Child Poverty Action Group publish a *Child Support Handbook* (price £12.95 but only £3.50 to benefit claimaints).
Telephone: 0171 837 7979.

SECTION III

SOMEONE ELSE'S CHILD

CHAPTER TEN

ADOPTION

Adoption usually brings to mind a picture of a lovely newborn baby being handed into the care of an adoring young couple, who have been yearning for a child of their own and will care for the child until he or she grows into adulthood, just as though they had been the birth parents. Adopting a child can sometimes be like that, but is not in the majority of cases nowadays. The increased use of contraceptives, together with the high rate of abortion, means that there are fewer unplanned babies. Changes in the attitude of society to the single mother, plus the availability of state benefits, have meant that it is easier for mothers to bring up children on their own. Within living memory, to be an unmarried mother was to experience shame and ostracism, which even extended to the unfortunate child. Today an unmarried mother may keep her child if she so wishes without the same fear of society's disapproval.

There is, however, no shortage of couples anxious to adopt, so that increasing numbers of older children are currently being adopted. It is not uncommon for families to adopt two or more brothers and sisters, or children with disabilities.

To adopt a child is to take that child into your family. It should be just as important to you and to the child as giving birth to your own child. Once the adoption order has been made by the court, the child becomes part of the family into which he or she has been adopted. Links with birth parents, natural brothers and sisters, grandparents and other members of the extended birth family are usually, but not always, completely severed. The new parents of an adopted child take on all the legal and moral responsibilities towards that child that they would have had if he or she had been their natural child.

Obviously, since adoption is such an exciting and important step for a child and for the adopters, great care has to be taken and a full investigation made before an adoption order can be contemplated.

Adoption orders can only be made by the courts, and then after the most detailed enquiry has been made into whether it will be in the best interests of the child.

Who can Adopt?

You do not have to be a married couple to adopt – but it helps. Married couples are preferred because they have made a public commitment to permanency in their relationship and that gives a better chance of stability for the child.

However, it is the fact that some children, often those described as having special needs, are successfully adopted by, for example, unmarried women, divorced women or young widows. There are other cases in which adoption by a single person may be the best option for a child – an example would be in the case of a widowed stepfather with whom the child had been living before the mother's death.

People who wish to adopt a child must be over the age of 21 and must be viewed as capable of meeting the needs of a child. These are the basic requirements.

Babies

Because so many people wish to adopt, many adoption agencies have their own additional requirements which applicants must meet, and this applies particularly in the case of babies. These requirements vary according to the particular agency, but one example is that most agencies will only consider placing a healthy baby with married couples who can prove that they are unable to have a child of their own.

Some agencies will not consider an applicant for a baby if he or she is over the age of 40, and the limit can even be as young as 35. Some agencies will not accept anyone who has been divorced, and most expect a marriage to have lasted for at least three years before they will consider a couple as suitable adopters for a baby.

Children with Special Needs

As you would expect, healthy babies are always very easy to place, so that agencies can afford to be as particular as they choose about the requirements which have to be met by prospective adopters, which may seem rather daunting if you are over 35, have been divorced or have not been married for as long as three years.

If you are thinking of adoption, you do not need to be particularly well off financially, although naturally the agency will want to ensure that you can afford to support a child. In some special cases, it may be possible to get an allowance to help meet the costs of bringing up a child, although normally adopters receive no payment for caring for the child, unlike foster carers.

Where do you begin?

If you want to adopt a child, you must first contact an adoption agency. A list is supplied at the end of this chapter. Adoption is such an important and irrevocable step in the life of a child that an adoption order can only be made by a civil court. Local authority social services departments and voluntary adoption agencies all have adoption panels. Members of these panels include experienced professional people and ordinary non-professional people. Before recommending to a court that a child should be adopted, local authorities and agencies take advice from their adoption panels. If a child is being adopted by a step-parent or other family member, the local authority provides a report for the assistance of the court.

All reports to the court in adoption proceedings will contain information about the history and family background of the child who is to be adopted, with similar details about the prospective adopters. Medical reports must be provided by prospective adopters, because anyone who is suffering from a condition which is life-threatening or disabling, in a way which could make it difficult to care for a child, is unlikely to be considered as an adopter. The information provided to the court is, obviously, completely confidential, which can mean that if you are adopting a child you could find that there will be some reports which you will not be allowed to see.

What happens if the Natural Parent does not Consent?

The natural parents of the child must consent to the adoption. However, if they refuse to do so, the court can sometimes dispense with their consent. In some cases there is a real dispute about whether or not a particular child should be adopted.

CASE STUDY

Marianne, who is an unmarried eighteen year old, gives birth to Louis. She decides that she can't give Louis the stability and material advantages that he could be given by adopters, so agrees that he should be placed by the local authority with Martin and Carole with a view to his being adopted by them. Before the matter comes to court for the adoption order to be made, Marianne changes her mind. Louis has been with Martin and Carole since shortly after his birth and they already love him as their own child. They are frantic with worry about losing him. The test for the court is whether Marianne's refusal to consent to the adoption is reasonable. In all the circumstances of Marianne's case, the court decides that her refusal to consent is not reasonable. It can then go on to make the adoption order, dispensing with Marianne's consent.

CASE STUDY

Rachel and Joe are the divorced parents of Jesse, who is six years old. They separated when Jesse was three. Rachel has married again. Her new husband Bernard wants to adopt Jesse. But Joe does not agree that Jesse should be adopted. He does not see Jesse on a regular basis, but he has had contact on two or three occasions a year since he and Rachel separated. He sends Jesse birthday and Christmas presents. Sometimes he telephones him. Jesse does not remember living with his father but he does know who he is. In all the circumstances, the court decides that Joe's consent to Jesse's adoption by Bernard is not being unreasonably withheld. Consequently, the adoption order is refused.

Once again, remember that every case is decided by the court on its own facts, and no two cases have identical facts. These case studies are merely examples of what might be decided.

The consent of a natural parent to a proposed adoption might also be withheld in a case where the child has been removed from home and taken into care because there were serious concerns about risks to the child in the home situation. The first objective of local authorities and courts must be to keep children in their birth families whenever it is possible to do so. Social services have a legal duty to give families support in an effort to help them stay together.

But there are still many cases where massive support has been offered by social services and has failed to improve the home situation sufficiently for it to be in a child's interests to remain with or return home to birth parents. Or the child may have been so seriously abused, emotionally, physically or sexually, that the risk of a return home cannot possibly be taken. In cases like that the local authority may ask the court for permission to place the child for adoption. Often the parents will not consent to this.

Where a parent refuses consent the court has to look at the situation from the point of view of a 'reasonable parent'. Would a reasonable parent, knowing all the facts and acting in the best interests of the child, have given consent to the adoption? If so, the court can say that the parental consent is being unreasonably withheld. This means that the adoption order can be made even though the natural parent does not consent.

Can an Adopted Child Contact the Birth Family?

In recent years there has been an increasing tendency for 'open adoption' orders to be made. These orders have been called open adoption orders because the link with the child's birth family has not been completely cut. Obviously, the older the child, the more memories of his or her birth family there will be. In many cases, even where a child has been seriously neglected or abused in the natural family, there will still be a strong emotional link with a parent or other relative, such as a grandparent.

In some of those cases, the court has taken the view that it is in the interests of that child to preserve the link with that family member, even after an adoption order has been made. The link could be through contact by letters or birthday and Christmas cards or gifts. It might even take the form of face to face contact once or twice a year.

There are cases where contact will be much more significant. It may be decided by the court, for example, that ongoing contact should take place several times a year between brothers or sisters who have been separately adopted. The test will always be what would be in the best interests of the children concerned, but it is not unknown for the court to consider that contact between siblings is of overriding importance in a case where the children have close emotional links.

This can pose considerable problems. Not every couple wishing to adopt a child is prepared for that child's natural family to have ongoing contact with the child, however infrequent that contact may be. While prospective adopters are sometimes prepared to agree to and even encourage inter-sibling contact, the suggestion of contact with a natural parent or grandparent can be less easy to take. This in turn means that finding a suitable match of prospective adopters for the child can be trickier for the adoption agency.

Nor are experts by any means in agreement about the benefits of open adoption. Some firmly believe that ongoing contact with the birth family, no matter how minimal, can undermine the child's ability to form a positive new relationship with the adopting family and so endanger the success of the whole enterprise.

In considering this dilemma, the court will take the view that the most important objective is to support the new family relationship. Where the birth parents wish to retain direct contact, free consent to that must be given by the child (if he or she is old enough to understand) and the new family. However, where the adoptive parents are against the contact, their view will often prevail. In the case of older children, who have been adopted out of families with whom they have formed a close bond, the issues need particularly careful judgment and the child's view will become correspondingly significant.

Telling the Child

In cases where a child has been adopted at such a young age that he or she will have no memory of birth family, it is extremely important that the child should grow up with the knowledge that he or she has been adopted. In the past, it sometimes happened that a child would grow to adolescence, even adulthood, without becoming aware that he or she had been adopted by the parents who had always been regarded as birth parents.

The adoptive parents would probably have withheld the facts from their child from the best possible motives, perhaps because they could not bring themselves to break the news, perhaps even thinking that the child need never discover the truth. But so far as the child was concerned, the discovery that he or she had in fact been adopted could come as the most profound shock, almost invariably triggering off an emotional reaction which might result in deep psychological effects. The saddest cases of all would be where a child first heard of his adoption through the taunt of another child.

Few adoptive parents nowadays have not been counselled as to the way in which they should approach the question of the adoption with their child. In the case of an adoption of a baby or toddler, undoubtedly the best and easiest way is to bring the child up with the realisation that he or she has been adopted. Telling a child the story of how he or she was specially chosen by the parents is a positive line of approach.

One wise and experienced family judge, himself a grandfather, always instructed adoptive parents that their child was to have two birthday celebrations – one on the birth date and one on the date when the adoption order had been made. That immediately made adoption something which other children would wish had happened to them too. Needless to say, children brought to him for an adoption order who were old enough to understand the recommendation were always very much in favour of it!

Older children who are adopted will usually have a 'life story book' which has been prepared by a social worker. The book will contain photographs and information about their birth families and a history of how the child came to be adopted.

Finding the Birth Family

Where there is no ongoing contact with the birth family, the time may come when an adopted child wants to know more about it. Equally, birth parents may wish to establish later contact. Great care must be taken to preserve confidentiality in these situations because, for example, the birth mother may have made a new life for herself and never told her husband or children about the adopted child.

To find out information about a child's birth family, you should approach the Adoption Contact Register (address at the end of the chapter) which is organised by the Office of Population Censuses and Surveys. This enables birth parents, and adopted children once they reach the age of eighteen, to apply for the information necessary to make contact with one another. Such information is provided only when both parents and child agree that it should be.

Although such curiosity is natural, there are situations where a child, or his or her natural parents, will not wish to be contacted. The child may feel such loyalty to the adoptive parents that he/she does not wish to contact the birth parents. Or a mother, who had her child by a relationship prior to her marriage and of which her husband knows nothing, may be fearful of the impact on her life were the child to make contact.

It is right that people in vulnerable positions should have their right to privacy protected. In order to afford such protection, it is proposed that, in future, the birth parents and other relatives will be able to record on the Register that they do not wish to be contacted. The adopted child will have the same right. Where such an indication has been given, no information will be obtainable from the Register.

Adoption agencies will have three main functions concerning contact:

(a) to make arrangements to keep open the possibility of voluntary contact after adoption;

(b) to consult birth parents about whether they wish to be kept informed about their child's progress and to counsel them as to the benefits and disadvantages;

(c) to counsel the adoptive parents and ascertain their wishes and those of the child.

Adopted children have the right, once they have reached the age of eighteen, to apply to the Registrar General for the information they need to obtain copies of their birth certificates. Full birth certificates normally contain the names and addresses of the birth parents at the date of birth.

Difficult Questions

From time to time there are worrying stories in the media about the approach to adoption taken by some local authorities. A toddler may be uprooted from the only family he/she has ever consciously known simply because the child and the family are not an ethnic match. It is on such occasions that the suspicion arises that a doctrinaire approach is overriding considerations of what may be in the best interests of a particular child.

CASE STUDY

Ahmed's parents, originally from Pakistan, were living in London when he was born. Ahmed was taken into care by the local authority shortly after his birth due to serious concerns about the risk to him in the care of his natural parents. He was placed with foster parents, Syl and Bert, who were English. The local authority had intended that this should be a short-term placement, since, it was their policy that children should be placed in families which were an ethnic 'match' for the child. In fact, no alternative placement was found and Ahmed remained with Syl and Bert until he was three years old. At that stage the local authority decided to ask the court for permission to look for adoptive parents for him. Although Syl and Bert had by this time become so fond of Ahmed that they wished to put themselves forward to be considered is his adopters, the local authority made it clear that, because of their ethnic match policy, they would not consider the foster parents as possible adopters. Syl and Bert challenged this decision in court and it was decided that Ahmed, having known no other family, looked upon them as his parents. In his interests, Syl and Bert should be allowed to adopt him.

Nobody would argue against the view that children should be matched as closely as possible with prospective adoptive families. It has always been a requirement of the law that those responsible for adoption should have regard, so far as practicable, to any wishes of a child's parents or guardians in regard to the religious upbringing of the child.

The legislation on adoption does not contain any references to ethnicity or culture. But in recent years these are matters which have usually been taken into account. Obviously it makes sense to have them as considerations, but there is a suspicion that on occasions they are given too much weight, so that a balanced overall judgement on the suitability of an adoptive placement can be put at risk.

It is being proposed that in future legislation there will be a broad requirement to consider ethnicity and culture when trying to match a child with an adoptive family.

But although ethnicity and culture are factors to be considered, they should not necessarily be more influential than any other factors.

There has been no research which conclusively demonstrates that children adopted by people of a different ethnic group will necessarily encounter problems of identity or prejudice later in life. Clearly, any preferences expressed by the birth parents or the child, if old enough, should be given weight among other factors covering all the characteristics, circumstances and needs of the child. The most important assessment should be the ability of the proposed adopters to help and support that child through all the challenges he or she will face in life, rather than overstress any risk of difficulty which might arise from ethnic background.

Overseas Adoption

Increased and dramatic media coverage of disaster areas in Third World countries has brought the haunting little faces of starving or abandoned children right into our livingrooms. The collapse of communist regimes in Eastern Europe, with the consequent media focus on the plight of children in war-ravaged areas has sparked off fresh concern. Many couples have offered homes to children from overseas, only to be confronted by the huge legal obstacles which have to be surmounted in the case of overseas adoption. If you want to adopt a child from overseas, it is necessary for a home study to be carried out by your local authority. But you will have to make your own arrangements for the adoption, as there is no adoption agency in Britain which brings children from overseas into the country.

In each country there will be legal requirements which have to be met before a child is removed. Moreover, Home Office immigration rules will also have to be complied with before the child can be brought here.

Even though you may have legally adopted the child in the country of his or her birth, it will almost always be necessary for the whole adoption process to be gone through again before a British court. It all takes a long time, and a great deal of hard work, money and patience.

You have to remember that, no matter how sad the plight of the child in his own country may seem to you, many governments are far from enthusiastic about allowing their children to be exported. There is also the moral question of whether it is always in a child's interest to be uprooted to a foreign county. That having been said, many families have successfully adopted children from overseas and no doubt many more would like to consider it.

If you are thinking of adopting a child from overseas you should contact British Agencies for Adoption and Fostering (BAAF), address given at the end of this chapter.

Useful Addresses

British Agencies for Adoption and Fostering (BAAF)
11 Southwark Street
London SE1
Telephone: 0171 593 2000
(for information on all aspects of adoption including overseas adoption)

NCH Action for Children
85 Highbury Park
London N5 lUD
Telephone: 0171 226 2033

Catholic Children's Society (Crusade of Rescue)
73 St Charles Square
London W10 6EJ
Telephone: 0181 969 5305

Post-Adoption Centre
5 Torriano Mews
Torriano Avenue
London NW5 2RZ
Telephone: 0171 284 0555

Parents for Children (older and hard-to-place children)
41 Southgate Road
London N1 3JP

Adoption Contact Register
ONF
The General Register Office
Adoption Section
Smedley Hydro
Trafalgar Road
Southport PR8 2HH
Telephone: 0151 471 4831

CHAPTER ELEVEN

FOSTERING

If you are thinking of becoming a foster carer, it is as well to remember that you need rather special qualities. A foster parent is someone who becomes a parent but only for a period of time. You have to care for a child just as though the child were your own, but you must always keep in mind that he/she is not. This can be a lot harder than it sounds. Through caring for a child, you are quite likely to become attached and feel as though you were the parent and the longer the fostering placement lasts the stronger that feeling will become. But if fostering is a temporary arrangement – even though it may be long-term – so foster carers have to be on their guard against making too much of an emotional commitment to the children in their care.

There are all sorts of reasons why a child might need foster care – from the child whose mother has had to go into hospital for a short time to the child whose parents are, for some reason, unable to carry on as parents, and who needs a long-term substitute family. Another common situation is where a child is suffering from some kind of permanent disability and needs foster care for short periods in order to give his or her own parents a break. Depending on the circumstances you can care for a foster child for a period which can be as brief as a couple of days or last for years, even throughout the whole of his or her childhood.

Sometimes there are close relatives who can care for children in these situations, but of course this is not always possible. The relatives may live a long way away from the parents, or have jobs or other commitments which make it impossible for them to offer assistance. However, where members of the extended family can help, it is possible for them to become approved foster carers, and they can then receive financial and other kinds of support from the local authority.

Another aspect of being a foster carer which requires careful thought is that children in foster care will need to see as much of their natural parents as possible. This will often mean that the natural parents will be visiting and/or making telephone calls to the foster home on a regular basis. So obviously if you are going to be a foster carer, you will have to be prepared to co-operate with natural parents to ensure that the children keep their ties with them.

Private Fostering

If you are going to look after a child aged under sixteen for more than 28 days, and you are not a relation or legal guardian of that child, you will be acting as the child's foster carer. It makes no difference whether or not you are being paid any money for looking after the child. So if you are planning to look after someone else's child for more than 28 days you must notify your local authority social services department.

You should notify the social services department not less than six weeks and not more than thirteen weeks before the date when you will be taking over the care of the child. The parents, the proposed foster carers, and anyone else who has been involved in making the arrangements, all have a legal duty to inform social services about the plan.

Of course, a situation could arise where you are asked to look after a child for more than 28 days in some emergency and it would not be possible for you to give six weeks' notice. The child's parents might have been injured in a road accident, for example. In an emergency like that the local authority must be informed within 48 hours.

The local authority can forbid someone to foster. It can also make conditions about, for example, the number of children in a foster home, or the ages or sexes of the children being fostered. If social workers consider that a home is unsuitable for any reason, they can remove a child who is being fostered privately. When children are being privately fostered they are visited regularly by a social worker who makes sure that they are being properly cared for.

Local Authority Fostering

There are two types of situation in which local authorities will foster children in England and Wales.

1. When parents are unable to look after a child themselves for any reason, such as lack of housing, illness or other family problems, they can ask their local authority for help. The social workers will find a temporary foster home for the child, and the parents will be able to take their child back home whenever they wish to do so. If the foster placement has been for any length of time, it is usual for the return to the parents to be planned together by the parents, the foster carers, the children's social worker, and the child himself or herself, if old enough. This means that the move can be made with as little disruption to the child as possible.

2. If a child is being neglected or ill-treated in some may in his or her own home, the local authority must investigate and must take the case to court, if that is the only, way to protect the child from significant harm. If the court is satisfied that the child is suffering or is likely to suffer significant harm in the home, and can only be protected by an order, it makes an order which places the child in the care of the local authority. When a care order has been made the natural parents will not be able to remove the child from care unless the local authority agrees or the court makes another order.

The Rules

There have to be very strict rules about any foster placement. The local authority, has to visit any proposed foster home, make enquiries about it and approve it before children can be placed there. After the child has been placed, a social worker will visit at regular intervals to check that the child is happy and well cared for. A child has to have a medical check before moving into a foster home, and will have regular medical checks while in the foster home.

The local authority has to make a written agreement with the foster parents about such things as the arrangements for the child's health, what contact there is to be with the child's birth family and what financial support is to be provided for the child. The local authority also has to give the foster carers written information about the child's background, health and mental and emotional development.

If you are going to be a foster carer you have to sign an agreement which promises that you will:

(a) care for the child as though he or she were a member of your own family;

(b) notify the local authority of any serious illness or other serious matter concerning the child;

(c) comply with any arrangements made for social workers to visit your home;

(d) notify the local authority of any change of address or any change in the people who live at your address;

(e) allow the local authority to remove the child on request;

(f) not use corporal punishment against the child and not disclose any confidential information.

What about Payment?

If you are going to foster a child privately, and you are going to be paid for doing so, you will be making your own arrangements with the birth parents about what the payments should be. When you foster a child who is being looked after by a local authority you will be paid an allowance for feeding, clothing and looking after the child. If you foster a child who needs special care, for example one with a mental or physical disability, you may be paid a special allowance which takes the additional responsibility into account. Local authorities do not all pay the same allowances for foster placements, so you would have to find out what the rates are in the particular area in which you are living.

What Kind of People are Chosen to be Foster Carers?

Many different kinds of people become foster carers. The main requirement is that they can give a child a loving and secure home. Some foster carers already have children of their own. Some are older people whose children are grown up. Some do not have any children of their own. You can foster one child or several at a time, you can specialise in babies, toddlers or teenagers. Foster carers have all sorts of jobs and all sorts of homes.

When social workers are trying to find a foster home for a particular child, they will have in mind the kind of cultural background and religious beliefs in which the child has been brought up. They will try to match these as far as humanly possible in the foster home, so that the child will find much that is already familiar.

People become foster carers for all kinds of reasons. Maybe their friends have enjoyed being foster carers. They may have read articles about foster caring or seen television programmes which attracted them. Or they may have replied to advertisements for foster carers in the media.

If you have had no previous experience of fostering, you will probably be put in touch with other foster carers, so that you can discuss what it is like to foster a child before you actually, have one placed with you. In many areas there are foster care associations which organise meetings for their members. You will always have the support of the social workers from your local authority, who have responsibility for any child placed with you.

Ideally, fostering is meant to be a partnership between the foster carers, the social workers, the birth parents and the child, if he or she is old enough to take part in decision making. It is challenging and, as always, when it comes to caring for children, hard work. But if you love children, want to help those in trouble, *and* can love and let go, it is a most rewarding occupation.

How do you Begin?

If you are interested in becoming a foster parent, you can find out more about fostering from the social services department of your local authority. The number will be in the telephone directory. Just ring up and say that you are interested in finding out more about becoming a foster parent. You may be asked a few questions about yourself and your family over the telephone. After that, a social worker will probably visit you or invite you to come for a chat about what fostering involves. Obviously, it will be necessary for someone from social services to check your home to see what sort of accommodation you have to offer a child or children. Social services will want to know who lives in your home and will have to ask many other, rather personal, questions about your family life. You may be asked to provide the names of people who will provide you with a character reference.

Useful Addresses

The National Foster Care Association
87 Blackfriars Road
London SE1 8HA
Telephone: 0171 620 6400

British Agencies for Adoption and Fostering (BAAF)
11 Southwark Street
London SE1
Telephone: 0171 593 2000

Catholic Children's Society (Crusade of Rescue)
73 St Charles Square
London W10 6EJ
Telephone: 0181 969 5305

Your local authority social services department (in the telephone directory).

SECTION IV

FAMILIES IN CRISIS

CHAPTER TWELVE

CHILD ABUSE

It is no exaggeration to say that the most horrifying crimes committed in our society are those against children. We are revolted by such crimes principally because children are, by definition, innocent and defenceless. The younger the child the more the protection and love which ought to be given to him or her by adults. Children are naturally trusting and affectionate. A betrayal of that trust must be one of the hardest things in the world to forgive.

In recent years, when people hear it alleged that a child has been abused, they automatically seem to think of sexual abuse. This is not surprising, in view of the publicity which sexual abuse of children has received over the last decade or so. But children can, of course, be abused in ways other than sexually. They can have harm inflicted upon them by physical abuse which appears to have nothing to do with sexuality. Appalling cases where children are subjected to the most terrifyingly violent assaults are distressingly familiar. Neglect of a child is another form of abuse and the 'home alone' cases now regularly reported in the news are making people more aware of this. Cases of neglect do seem to be occurring with greater frequency than in the past. This may be due, as with other forms of child abuse, to the fact that increasing numbers of children are living in households where one of the parental figures, and particularly the father, is not the natural parent. It may be due to economic deprivation or unemployment, factors which can lead to feelings of depression and hopelessness and a lack of ability to cope with the demands of bringing up a family. It can simply be due to sheer ignorance of what the basic minimum needs of a child are. A more subtle form of abuse, but one which can be as damaging as physical abuse, is emotional abuse. We will be returning to this topic later in the chapter.

Sexual Abuse

Children are sexually abused at all ages, even as babies. Abuse can happen to any child, boy or girl, rich or poor, and the abuser can be male or female. Sadly, the abuser is frequently a member of the child's own family or a family friend.

Does sexual abuse of children occur more frequently now than in the past? Or is it that society is more vigilant and so more instances come to light? Or that there is more help available and more victims are prepared to speak up? Has the proliferation of pornographic material relating to children in recent years had an effect on the unstable personalities of potential abusers? Does the publicity given to child abuse in the media have the effect of encouraging further abuses?

Experts argue interminably about these questions and no doubt will continue to do so. What is certain is that, even fifteen years ago, court cases in which allegations of child abuse were involved were comparative rarities; now they have become depressingly common.

The Cleveland Report

At the time when it was being recognised that sexual abuse of children was much more common than had been imagined, there was an unfortunate backlash of overreaction on the part of some social workers and medical practitioners. While it might be understandable that professionals were anxious to remove children who were at real risk, the consequences of this overreaction could be and often were extremely damaging to the children concerned.

Matters came to a head in 1987, when public concern was aroused by events which had taken place in Cleveland. In May and June of that year, an unprecedented number of cases of sexual abuse of children had been diagnosed at the Middlesbrough General Hospital and many children had been summarily removed from their homes by social workers as a result.

Parents, nurses, the police and MPs voiced their protests and acute anxiety about what was happening. The matter became one of public debate. In July, it was announced in parliament that there would be a statutory enquiry into the matter.

The Findings

The enquiry lasted for 24 days and the report was published in the summer of 1988. Evidence was given by parents, paediatricians, psychiatrists, social workers, police officers, MPs and other people with an interest in the matter.

Although it acknowledged that doctors and social workers had been motivated by the best of intentions, the enquiry came to the conclusion that things had gone very wrong in Cleveland in the Spring of 1987. In a period of five months, two hospital doctors who had become interested in the question of sexual abuse of children had diagnosed abuse in 121 children from 57 families.

Children had been referred to the doctors in various ways. Some were brought by social workers as a result of allegations or suspicions that they were being abused. Some were referred by general practitioners, health visitors or community medical officers. Some children were referred who had attended at the outpatients department of the hospital with problems totally unconnected with sexual abuse. In many cases, brothers and sisters, or other children connected in some way with a child where abuse had been diagnosed, were also referred to one of the doctors, who diagnosed that they too had been abused.

Most of those children were separated from their families and their homes. By the time the report was published most had in fact returned home. The enquiry report criticised the doctors for their over-confident approach and it criticised social services and the police. It came to the firm conclusion that the desperately unhappy experiences of many of the children concerned should not be allowed to occur again. To that end the report made certain recommendations.

The Recommendations

The Cleveland Report emphasised the danger which can arise for professionals that, when looking to the welfare of children believed to be the victims of sexual abuse, the children themselves, as individuals, might be overlooked and be treated as objects of concern instead of as individuals.

The report went on to make important recommendations, which should be followed in all cases where sexual abuse of children has been alleged. Unfortunately, years later, many of these recommendations are still not being followed, with damaging results for the children concerned and their families.

Parents

The recommendations so far as parents were concerned were as follows.

1. That they should be treated in the same way as the family of any other child referred to social services. Sadly this does not always happen: in one case where an allegation of sexual abuse had been made, a social worker told the father that she could not bear to be in the same room as him.

2. Parents should be informed and, where appropriate, consulted at each stage of the investigation by the professional dealing with the child, whether medical, police or social worker. Parents are entitled to know what is going on, and to be helped to understand the steps which are being taken.

3. Social services should confirm all important decisions to parents in writing. Parents may not understand the implications of decisions made and they should have an opportunity to show the written decision to their lawyers.

4. Parents should always be advised of their rights of appeal or complaint in relation to any decisions made about them or their children.

5. Social services should always seek to provide support to the family during the investigation. Parents should not be left isolated and bewildered at this difficult time.

6. Case conferences (where all the professionals involved – social workers, teachers, the GP and the police – meet to discuss the case) are held at regular intervals. Parents should be invited to attend for all or part of every conference unless, in the view of the chairman of the conference, their presence would prevent a

full and proper consideration of the child's interests.

What happened in Cleveland was an extreme situation. But it has by no means been uncommon for professionals to overreact where sexual abuse is suspected. It is also more than regrettable that, even though it is now more than ten years since the publication of the Cleveland Report, there are still cases in which guidelines set out are not being followed by some police officers, social workers and psychiatrists.

False Allegations

Since the problem of the sexual abuse of children came to public attention, there has been an extremely worrying development. In cases where parents have separated and the parent with care of the child does not wish the other parent to have contact, it has become all too easy to allege that the child is being sexually abused. This is particularly so in the case of very young children. Unfortunately, there is no doubt whatsoever that these false allegations are frequently made by parents. The parent making the allegation, usually the mother, almost invariably achieves the first aim of making the allegation, in that contact with the other parent is terminated, or is only permitted under the supervision of some other adult.

Most local authorities, hard pressed by financial restraints, are neither willing nor able to provide such supervision for regular contact. The parent making the allegation will object to every supervisor suggested by the other parent, so that eventually the parent against whom the allegation has been made will either be compelled to pay for supervision by an independent social worker or not be allowed to see the child.

The damage done to a child by a false allegation like this can be incalculable. First, there is the loss of the relationship with the falsely accused parent. Even if the allegation is eventually proved to be false, months will have passed while it was being investigated.

During that time any contact between parent and child will have taken place in the totally artificial environment of supervision. Investigations will be going on. The child may be interviewed by police officers and social workers, perhaps on more than one occasion.

An intimate medical examination, extremely distressing to the child, may take place. There may be more than one physical examination. A psychiatrist or child psychologist may be asked to investigate. It is not uncommon for a young child to have several sessions with such experts.

It has to be said that the quality and expertise of the various professionals who interview children in these situations varies tremendously. The real experts are sensitive and objective. They do not approach the interviews with their minds already made up as to the truth of the allegations. They do not call the interviews 'disclosure sessions', implying that they expect to obtain confirmation of already formed opinions. They do not ask the child questions which suggest the answers which fit in with their preconceptions.

Unfortunately for many children and many parents, there are professionals who fall far short of this standard. These are the social workers, doctors and child psychiatrists who accept without question allegations made by parents in situations where, with minimal investigation, it would be possible to discern the residual bitterness which remains over the breakdown of a relationship, and which should automatically put professionals on their guard.

The type of question asked by professionals overkeen to obtain 'disclosure' is that of the social worker producing an anatomically explicit male doll to a four year old. Helping the child to undress the doll, the social worker prompted, 'He looks a little bit like Daddy, doesn't he?' The child examined the doll thoughtfully, then said, 'Not really; my Daddy's got a moustache.'

The American Experience

False allegations of sexual abuse of children in the divorce context have become so widespread in America that the problem is now known as 'SAID – sexual allegations in divorce'. Such allegations, when made in the context of an acrimonious separation of the parents, are now treated with great reserve in the United States. It should be obvious that caution ought to be exercised by professionals when the allegation that the child has been abused by the parent with contact initially comes from a separated parent with care of the child.

But the tragedy for some children and their parents is that it has taken some years for lawyers and other professionals to realise that allegations that a child is being sexually abused can be and are being made falsely in order to exclude a parent from the child's life.

When the allegation is false, not only does the child lose a parent, he or she also has to grow up in the care of a parent who promotes the belief that sexual abuse did take place, with all the resultant consequences to emotional stability in adolescence and adulthood which that belief entails. Parents who inflict that burden on their own children for their own selfish ends must bear a responsibility which is quite as heavy as that of a parent who has actually sexually abused a child.

Not all parents who make false allegations of abuse against the other parent are fully aware of what they are doing, of course. For example, a mother who would really like to cut the father out of the child's life may misinterpret some perfectly innocent remark made by the child. She reports her suspicions to social services. Much will depend upon who speaks to the child. An over-zealous social worker, with little real knowledge of sexually abused children, can do irreparable damage by approaching discussion with the child in the wrong way. The social worker supports the mother's allegation and the mother, secretly delighted, convinces herself that it is not she who is curtailing the father's contact with the child but social services.

Young children are very suggestible. They can quickly learn, without understanding what they are being asked, that certain responses to questions from professionals are more welcome than others.

An assertion frequently made by professionals concerned with child abuse is that a young child always tells the truth, so that children must be believed. This ignores the fact, known to any parent of a young child, that children have vivid imaginations. They may be telling the truth in the sense that they believe what they say. But that does not necessarily mean that what they say is true.

One American researcher has recently come up with most disturbing findings. One of the experiments he conducted was with a class of five year old children in a school. He told the children that a man would be coming into the classroom and that this man would behave badly. Shortly afterwards a man entered the classroom and stayed for a few minutes. He did not do anything and he did not speak to the children. Afterwards the children were asked to describe what the man did.

Some of the children reported accurately that the man did nothing. But several of them recounted naughty things which he had done, in great detail. Because it had been suggested to them before he came that he would behave badly, they supplied details of his bad behaviour through their own imaginations. It is important to realise that they were not lying. They believed what they said.

An even more surprising result came from a second experiment, which was made with a number of young children from normal families. The children were interviewed on their own, and each was asked if she or he had ever had a finger caught in a mousetrap. Each child said that this had never happened.

Each child was interviewed in a neutral manner on several subsequent occasions. No suggestive questioning was used. They were simply asked again whether they had ever had a finger caught in a mousetrap. Some of the children began to say that it had happened and to supply details about the occasion.

One little boy constructed an elaborate account. He eventually told the interviewer that he and his brother had been playing in the cellar of the family home while their father was chopping wood. His brother, he said, had pushed him and he had fallen into a pile of chopped wood. A mousetrap had been concealed in the wood pile and he had caught his finger in it. He had been taken by ambulance to the hospital. His mother and father and brother had visited him in hospital.

The father of this child was asked to explain to him that all this had never happened and that he was imagining it. The child listened to his father, but the next time he was asked the question by an interviewer he recounted the same details and insisted that all this had actually happened to him. Clearly he believed that it had, and so he was speaking the truth.

These experiments cast some doubt on the assertion that all children must invariably be believed. If you substitute for the neutral questioning in the experiment the emotionally loaded questioning of a much loved parent who, consciously or unconsciously, wants to believe that abuse has occurred, it seems all too possible that a child can become convinced that abuse has taken place when it has not.

This means that professionals should be particularly careful to avoid coming to conclusions about abuse based on what a young child may be saying, in the absence of other evidence. They should be particularly on their guard where there is an acrimonious relationship between the child's parents.

Sometimes a medical examination of the child will prove conclusive, more often the result will be inconclusive. However, if a child is being abused there will normally be other signs of what is happening, perhaps in behaviour at school, possibly in some physical deterioration.

Emotional Abuse

The making of a false allegation that a child has been sexually abused is one form of emotional abuse of the child. Emotional abuse is not, of course, so easily detected as physical or sexual abuse, but it can certainly be as damaging to the child.

It is well known that sexual abusers also exert emotional abuse over their victims. Almost invariably, the sexual abuse is accompanied by threats of what will happen to the child if the abuse is ever disclosed. These can range from threats that the child will be believed to be telling lies, to threats of violence and even murder. The child is frequently threatened that he or she will be taken into care and will not be allowed to live at home ever again, or that he or she will be responsible for breaking up the family.

Children who are being abused in any way by a parent very often still retain feelings of love for that parent. They are placed in an intolerable situation. They may not want to get the abusing parent into trouble. They may not even be aware that they are being abused. Many children, particularly young children, simply assume that what is happening to them happens to all children.

Above all, an abused child may desperately want to stay at home. He or she wants the abuse to stop, of course, but the threat of being taken into care may prevent any disclosure of what is happening. Sadly, lawyers and other professionals are all too familiar with cases where children who have been abused will withdraw the disclosures which they have made just because they want so much to return home.

Sometimes, when there has been abuse by a parent and that parent is prepared to acknowledge this and apologise to the child, it is possible that they may be reunited. Usually, this will mean that a period of months will be spent in family therapy to ensure that the child will be fully protected and feel safe before the return home can take place.

Children as Weapons

Children can be emotionally abused in situations where there is no form of physical abuse. Parents with care who persistently make difficulties about a child seeing the other parent are emotionally abusing their children, whether they realise it or not.

Similarly, it is emotional abuse of a child for one parent to denigrate the other to the child. Most parents who allow themselves to criticise the child's other parent would be quite horrified to be told that they are abusing the child. But they are undoubtedly doing just that.

The important thing for parents to remember is that relationships may founder, but parenthood lasts for life. If they can only make themselves civil to one another for the sake of their children, the benefits to the children will be huge. And they may even learn to like one another again.

What should you do if you Suspect a Child is being Abused?

Most of us are reluctant to interfere in other people's lives, but children do need the protection of adults. If you have reason to believe that a child is being abused in some way you should contact the social services department of your local authority. Social workers will then check on the situation. You need not worry that your name will be disclosed.

Signs to Look for if you Think a Child may be being Abused

Schools, doctors and social workers sometimes notice that a child is behaving in a way which makes them suspect that he or she may be being abused. Abused children may behave in sexually precocious ways with other children or with adults. They can become withdrawn or tearful. They can exhibit fear of adults. There are sometimes, of course, physical signs, such as otherwise unexplained soreness. Abused children often have nightmares. Someone who knows a child well, a family member, close friend of the family or teacher, may notice that the child's behaviour has changed in a worrying way, when there is no apparent reason for the change.

If there is a Court Case will the Child have to give Evidence?

If a child has been sexually abused and the abuser is charged with a criminal offence, the child sometimes has to give evidence about it. It has been recognised that this can be a traumatic experience for any child. Arrangements are now usually made for the child to give evidence in a room away from the court, by video link, in the presence some reassuring adult, such as the police officer in the case.

In a civil case, the child never has to give evidence. Any interview with the child, by a police officer, social worker or psychiatrist, which is designed to get the child to disclose details of the abuse, should be recorded on video, although it has to be said that this is not invariably done. The video can then be used in court proceedings.

Tragically, the sexual abuse of children appears to have become more common. Perhaps the only good result has been that facilities for helping abused children, through counselling and other therapy, are now widely available.

Useful Addresses

CRY-SIS Support Group (emotional support for parents of crying babies)
MM Cry-sis
London WC1N 3XX
Telephone: 0171 404 5011

PRAMS – Information and Support for Parents
Churchgate House
96 Churchgate
Stockport
Cheshire SKI 1YJ
Telephone: 061 477 0606

Childline
Telephone: 0800 1111

National Society for Prevention of Cruelty to Children (NSPCC)
Telephone: 0171 825 2500

CHAPTER THIRTEEN

CHILD ABDUCTION

'Please, please, get my baby back for me!' How many times have you heard that desperate plea and seen the tear-streaked face of some frantic mother on a television newscast or newspaper front page? Then there will be the photograph of the child who has been snatched by his or her estranged father, though of course estranged mothers sometimes snatch children too. But these incidents are always a time of enormous stress, not only for the parent from whom the child has been snatched but also, and even more importantly, for the unfortunate child concerned.

Kidnapping, at one time, was a crime which was almost invariably committed by people who were strangers to the child, and motivated by an intention to blackmail the parents of the victim into paying huge sums of money for the child's return. It was more common in America than here and the kidnapped child would often come from a very wealthy family.

The type of child-snatching with which we have become all too familiar over recent years is quite different. It usually happens when parents have separated, on acrimonious terms, and one parent (normally the father) does not accept that their child should live with the other. As the breakdown of parental relationships has become more common worldwide, international kidnapping – or child abduction as it is called legally – is happening more and more often.

CASE STUDY

Mervyn and Dee have been divorced. They were not able to agree with whom their seven year old twin girls, Lara and Petronella, should live. There was a court battle lasting two days, during which hurtful allegations were made on both sides. The court directed that the twins should live with Dee. Mervyn is a wealthy man. He likes his own way. The

twins are on his passport. One day he simply turns up at the
twins' school, tells the teacher that Dee has arranged that
he should collect the girls, drives them to the airport and
flies with them to a country which has no reciprocal arrangements with England about the enforcement of orders
relating to children.

The court here orders Mervyn to return the children to
Dee. He ignores the order. Dee is naturally extremely distressed. But Mervyn has forgotten one important thing. He
still has a home, a business and bank accounts in this country. In a case like this the court can, and will, make an order
that unless Mervyn obeys the order to return the children
his assets will be confiscated. Mervyn cannot afford to lose
the assets he has here, so he brings the twins back. On his
return he is arrested and brought before the court. He ignored the court order and so he is in contempt of court. He
is sent to prison for that offence.

In some cases a child may be wrongfully removed by one parent
from the care of the other when both parents are still in this country.
Any order then made by the court, will be easier to enforce if the
children have not been taken abroad. But, of course, it can happen
that the parent applying for the return of the child does not know
where the other parent has taken the child. In those circumstances
the court can make a 'seek and find' order, which instructs an officer
of the court (called a tipstaff) to make enquiries so that the child can
be traced.

In cases such as that, the court may give leave for details about
the child to be published in the media. This is exceptional, because
the general rule is that no details about a child concerned in any
court case may be published. But when other means of tracing a
child have failed, the publication of descriptions and photographs of
the missing child, and the parent who has taken him or her, may jog
the memory of some member of the public, enabling the child to be
traced.

The court can also order anyone who might be able to give some
information about the whereabouts of a missing child to come to
court to be asked what they know. Grandparents, other relatives or
close friends of the kidnapper, who could possibly have information
about the address to which the child has been taken, can be asked to
attend court, for example.

What do you do if you Believe your Child has been Abducted?

If you believe that your child has been kidnapped, and that there is a real risk that the other parent may be planning to take the child out of the country, the police should be told immediately. If the child is under the age of sixteen, you do not have to have a court order forbidding his or her removal before contacting the police, but if you do have an order, it must be shown to the police. The police will make contact with immigration officers and warn them to keep a watch for the child and the parent at seaports and airports. If the child is over the age of sixteen, you must get a court order before the police can act. If the case is really urgent, the court can make an order on the day you apply for it.

Before they do act, the police must satisfy themselves that the danger that the child will be taken out of the country is real and imminent.

It is important that you seek legal advice as soon as possible. Although solicitors are very busy people, if you explain the situation on the telephone, a solicitor will normally be able to see you very quickly.

Passports

You can also write to your regional office of the Passport Agency to ask the agency not to issue a passport for your child on the application of the other parent. The agency will usually need to see some court order which has been made about the child, but you do not normally have to have an order if you are an unmarried mother. If you believe that an application may have been made, or is soon to be made, you can telephone the agency.

If the other parent is not a British national, he or she may try to obtain a passport for the child from his or her own embassy, high commission or consulate in this country. You or your solicitor could write to request the officials of that embassy, high commission or consulate not to issue such a passport. They are not obliged to do what you ask, but they might do so voluntarily.

When a Child has been wrongfully taken Abroad

Sadly, it often happens that a child may have been spirited out of the country before anything can be done. With the increased speed and ease of travel between one country and another, problems of child abduction were becoming so common that the situation had to be tackled on an international basis. As a result, there are now two international Conventions which provide for the speedy return of children who have been wrongfully removed from the country where they usually live and taken to another state which recognises one of the Conventions. This now applies to many countries including the USA, Australia, Canada, New Zealand and most European countries.

CASE STUDY

Corinne and Des have been having problems in their marriage. Although they married in this country and their daughter Belle was born here, Corinne herself was born in Australia and all her family still live there. Corinne decides to take Belle with her to Australia. She knows that Des would never agree to this so, without telling Des, she books tickets and flies off with Belle to her family.

Corinne should not have taken Belle to Australia without the agreement of Belle's father, Des, or an order of the court. Des can go to court here and obtain an order that Corinne bring Belle back to this country. The court in Australia will enforce that order.

Incidentally, Corinne has behaved rather foolishly. A mother who is genuinely feeling lonely and isolated because her marriage has broken up and all her family are living in another country can apply to the court for permission to take her child or children to live with her in the country where her family are living, even where the children have been born and brought up here and their father is English. The court will then make a full enquiry, through a court welfare officer, as to whether or not it would be in the best interests of the children to go with the mother or not. It is not at all unusual for the court to give a mother – or indeed a father – permission to take the children to live abroad in such a case.

Again, it must be emphasised that every case turns on its own facts. There have been cases where the court refused such applications because it considered that it would not be in the children's interests to have their contact with the parent in England cut off or limited by geographical distance. Corinne would certainly have prejudiced her chances of obtaining court permission to remove Belle permanently by her behaviour in simply flying her off to Australia without even asking Belle's father about it.

We must hope that eventually these Conventions will be recognised throughout the world. Tragically, where a child has been removed to a country where neither Convention is recognised, there is nothing the courts here can do unless the parent who has snatched the child has assets here.

If the Child is taken to a Convention Country

A list of all the countries which belong to one or both of the two Conventions dealing with child abduction can be obtained from the Child Abduction Unit of the Lord Chancellor's department (address at the end of this chapter). If the child has been taken to one of those countries, staff at the unit will take brief details over the telephone and will send you a questionnaire to complete. When you send back the completed questionnaire you must send with it:

(a) copies of any court orders about the child which clearly show the court's seal;

(b) photographs of the child and the person who has taken the child;

(c) any other relevant information which might explain the circumstances of the removal or retention of the child or which may help in locating the child.

The Child Abduction Unit then makes a formal application for the return of the child, arranging for the details supplied on the completed questionnaire to be translated, if necessary. The formal application is sent, by airmail if appropriate, to the central authority of the country to which the child has been taken. The Unit will do all it can to speed matters up as far as humanly possible, but much will obviously depend upon the speed with which the other country deals with the case.

Under the Conventions no payment for legal proceedings in the country to which the child has been taken is normally required, although there are exceptions to this, particularly if the country concerned does not operate any legal aid system, as is the case, for example, with the USA. Again, the Child Abduction Unit will be able to supply information about likely costs, if any.

If the Child is taken to a Non-convention Country

If your child has been taken to a country which has not signed one of the Conventions, the situation is very much more complicated. If you cannot reach an amicable agreement with the other parent, or whoever has taken the child, you might have to instruct a lawyer in the country to which the child has been taken and institute legal proceedings in that country. The consular department of the Foreign and Commonwealth Office can give you a list of lawyers in any particular country who can correspond in English. Unfortunately, British consular officers in foreign countries cannot give legal advice or act as your legal representative.

Legal proceedings abroad may cost a great deal of money and British legal aid is not available for proceedings outside the country. There is a possibility that you might be able to get legal aid in the country to which the child has been taken, and any lawyer in that country should be able to advise about this. Another important point to remember is that foreign courts obviously apply their own laws. You might have a very good case in England, but the other parent could in fact have the law on his side in the country to which the child has been taken.

In some countries a mother does not have the same rights over a child as the father. Moreover, if you do not have the same social, cultural or religious background and it is your intention to bring the child back with you, these factors could well count against you in a foreign court. The lawyer of the country concerned will be able to advise you about all these matters.

Ways in which the Consular Department can help

The consular department may be able to help in the following ways, through British embassies and consulates abroad.

1. By asking the local authorities for help in tracing your child.

2. Once the child has been found, trying to obtain a report on his or her welfare – this can only be provided with the consent of the other parent and at your own cost.

3. If you decide to take proceedings, by asking the local court to deal with the case as quickly as possible.

4. Passing letters between you and the child (the other parent must consent).

5. Arranging for a room where you can spend time with the child privately (again the other parent must consent).

6. Informing the local authorities about any United Kingdom court orders which you might have obtained, provided the court agrees – these orders do not bind foreign courts but might be taken into consideration by them in reaching a decision.

Where a child is also a national of the country to which he or she has been taken (for example because the other parent is from that country), the authorities in that country are under no obligation to allow British consular staff to take any of the above steps.

If your Child has been abducted within the United Kingdom

Scotland and Northern Ireland have their own legal systems which are different from England and Wales. At one time these differences meant that a parent who had obtained a custody order for a child in England, for example, might be faced with the situation where the other parent took the child off to Scotland and obtained a custody order there. The English order might not be enforceable in Scotland and the Scottish order might not be enforceable in England.

The Family Law Act of 1986 put an end to these problems by

providing that the courts for the part of the United Kingdom with which the child has the closest long-term connection are the courts where orders may be obtained about that child. Orders made about the child by those courts will be enforced throughout the United Kingdom.

If you want to enforce an order which has been made about your child in your favour, you should apply to the court which made the order to register it in the court in which you wish to enforce it. The court will then send the papers to the appropriate court for registration.

Similar arrangements exist between the United Kingdom and the Isle of Man. The government departments and organisations which are listed at the end of this chapter are used to requests for urgent help or advice. You should not hesitate to contact them if your child has been abducted or if you believe there is a real risk of abduction.

Checklist

If you believe that there is a risk that the other parent might attempt to remove your child, it is a good idea to keep handy as much of the following information as you may have.

1. About the child:
    * full name, with date and place of birth;
    * passport number with date and place of issue;
    * physical description.

2. About the other parent:
    * full name and any other names by which parent has been known;
    * date and place of birth;
    * passport number with date and place of issue;
    * occupation;
    * probable date of departure;
    * flight information, if available;
    * details of ties with a foreign country – such as names, addresses and/or telephone numbers of family members;
    * friends or business contacts.

3. Copies of documents:
   - any agreements or court orders about the child;
   - child's birth certificate;
   - up to date photographs of the child;
   - the most recent photographs you have of the other parent.

You should seek advice from a solicitor as soon as possible. You can apply for an order prohibiting the other parent from removing the child from the country. Although the existence of the order does not guarantee that the other parent will not abduct the child, it make your position stronger in the event that an abduction does take place.

You should also warn the child's school and make sure they are clear about who can collect the child from school.

Criminal Offences

It is a criminal offence for a person connected with a child to take or to send a child under the age of sixteen out of the United Kingdom without the 'appropriate consent'. A person connected with a child might be a parent, a guardian, or someone who has a residence order in respect of the child. If the child's parents were not married to one another at the date of the child's birth, a man who is reasonably believed to be the father, is a person connected with the child.

If you have a residence order you are allowed, however, to remove the child or children from the United Kingdom for any period of less than one month, and you do not have to obtain the consent of anyone else to do so. This is just to ensure that a parent who has a residence order can take the child or children abroad for ordinary holidays without a lot of fuss.

'Appropriate consent' means the consent of the child's parents (if the father has parental responsibility), the guardian if there is one, or any person in whose favour there is a residence or custody order.

It is also a criminal offence, of course, for any other person, who is not connected with a child, to abduct that child.

Child abduction is a complicated subject. If at all possible it is best to consult a solicitor if you have a problem connected with a child who has been taken abroad, or who may be taken abroad wrongfully.

Counselling, Advice and Support

Reunite (address at the end of the chapter) is a charitable organisation the main aims of which are to advise on the recovery of abducted children and to prevent child abduction occurring in the first place. It gives advice and practical assistance to parents and lawyers whether the child has been taken to a Convention or non-Convention country.

Reunite can supply information on national and international law, and can give you the names of lawyers both here and abroad who are experienced in child abduction and who speak English. It can also advise about raising money to fund efforts to recover a child and about how to get assistance in bringing a child back. Reunite provides much-needed support for parents whose children have been abducted, by encouraging parents who have asked for advice to talk to other members of Reunite in their own area. They can also put a parent into contact with someone who has had experience in dealing with the country to which a child has been taken.

Useful Addresses

Child Abduction (a free booklet) is available from:
The Child Abduction Unit
Official Solicitor's Office
4th Floor
81 Chancery Lane
London WC2A 1DD
Telephone: 0171 9117127

Reunite
National Council for Abducted Children
PO Box 4
London WC1X 30X
Telephone: 0171 404 8356

Foreign and Commonwealth Office Consular Department
1 Palace Street
London FW1E 5HE

The United Kingdom Passport Agency
Clive House
Petty France
London SW1H 9HD

CHAPTER FOURTEEN

DOMESTIC VIOLENCE

We seem to live in an increasingly violent society. Distressingly, we constantly see and hear reports of horrific violence suffered by women at the hands of men, appalling violence suffered by children at the hands of adults, mindless violence against elderly people and the mentally or physically disabled, racial violence, even violence committed in the name of religion.

There are those who believe that the level of violence has not really increased. They argue, that because violence is given more prominence in the media today we are given the impression that the problem is a new one, but that it was always there. They point to the Victorian society depicted by Charles Dickens and to the Yorkshire Ripper of modern times who inherited his nickname from Victorian Jack.

Other people believe that the media have to bear a heavy responsibility for the level of violence in the present day. It is true that it would be difficult if not impossible to spend an evening watching television without having to view at least one scene of explicit violence. The producers of news bulletins no longer shrink from depicting the horrors of war or terrorism in the starkest possible detail. Fictional programme producers seem to believe that viewers are attracted by similarly explicit scenes.

The wide availability of video material depicting violence is another factor which some people believe has contributed to an acceptance of and desire for more violence in daily life. It is argued that huge sums of money are spent on advertising in the media, in the belief that exposure to advertisements influences people to spend money on the advertised product. If the media can persuade consumers to buy advertised items, does not that suggest that a media diet of violence must have an inevitable effect?

The judge who tried the two young boys who murdered two year old Jamie Bulger is reported to have expressed concern about the possibility that those children had been copying what they had seen on video film. The debate will probably never be resolved. But one thing is quite certain: there is a high level of violence in our society, and sadly much of that violence takes place in the home.

Battered Women

Many people seem to imagine that the sort of man who inflicts violence on his partner is likely to be an uneducated lout. Unfortunately, this stereotype is very misleading. Many men guilty of domestic violence are professional men, men who would be taken for perfect gentlemen by friends and business colleagues.

The women who experience the violence are very often reluctant to seek help or to tell anyone else about it. A bruised eye will be explained away as an accident with an open cupboard door. A limp resulting from a kick will have been caused by a fall downstairs. General practitioners and hospital casualty units are all too familiar with such explanations.

For many outsiders it is very easy to ask 'why doesn't she just leave him, or do something about it?', but many victims are reluctant to seek help because they truly believe the man will change. He may have apologised, told her that he did not understand what had come over him, promised that it will never happen again. She wants to believe that, she probably loves him, so she hides the problem.

Another factor in the woman's desire to conceal the violence will often be that she blames herself for it. Many women are told by husbands and boyfriends who beat them up that they have asked for it, it is their fault. Even though they should know how untrue that is, they come to believe it.

Shame and pride lead some battered women to cover up what has been happening. It is so humiliating to experience physical violence that they lose confidence and lose their respect for themselves. Frequently, the abusing man will tell the woman that no one will believe her, and she almost comes to accept that.

It is a sad fact of life that children who have lived with violence between parental figures in the home very often grow into adulthood to repeat the pattern. The first few years of our lives are vitally important in the development of our future personalities. A child learns about life from his or her own direct experiences and those experiences inevitably shape his or her adult attitudes and behaviour.

The sons of wife-beaters often develop their own adult relationships in the same pattern. Violence has been imprinted upon their subconscious as an integral part of their concept of a man's relationship with a woman.

The same can be true for the victims. A seventeen year old girl was giving evidence in court about her relationship with an older man who habitually inflicted violence on her. She was an attractive and obviously intelligent young girl. She was asked by the judge why on earth she had put up with the beatings.

She seemed almost surprised by the question, 'When I was little,' she said, 'my Dad always used to hit my Mum. So when my boyfriend hits me I know he loves me.'

It would be wrong to assume that domestic violence invariably means that a woman suffers at the hands of a man. There can be few lawyers practising in the field of family law who have not encountered cases where women have made a habit of assaulting their husbands or boyfriends.

It is of course even more humiliating for a man to have to admit that he is suffering violence at the hands of a woman. These cases are relatively uncommon, principally because the man is more powerful and physically stronger than the woman, so he can defend himself. Also, a man who is being abused in this way will be even more ashamed and unlikely to want to admit it.

Changing Attitude of the Police

Not many years ago the majority of police officers would have been dismissive of any incidents where domestic violence was involved. Injuries which would have been severe enough to warrant a criminal prosecution, had they been inflicted between strangers, would be disregarded if inflicted by a husband on a wife. This attitude had more than a little to do with the view of the law that a wife was the possession of her husband, to do with as he wished.

It is only very recently indeed that the courts have accepted that it is possible for a woman to be raped by her husband. For hundreds of years, the approach of the courts had been that the husband had an absolute right to sexual intercourse with his wife whenever he wanted it.

A leaflet which has recently been produced by the Metropolitan Police emphasises that domestic violence is a crime. Nobody has the right to assault you physically, sexually or emotionally. If you are being subjected to abuse, you should definitely call the police, who are committed to dealing with victims sympathetically and offering practical help and advice. In London alone 62 out of a total of 69 police stations have domestic violence units where men and women officers, who have received specialist training, are able to give advice and assistance to victims of domestic violence. More and more of these specialist units are being set up all over the country, and all police officers now have instructions to treat domestic assaults as criminal offences, and to prosecute the offenders if appropriate.

Aims of Domestic Violence Units

The objectives in setting up police domestic violence units are three-fold.

1. To provide a readily accessible service to victims and to assist them in making reasoned choices.

2. To help co-ordinate social, voluntary and caring agencies, to pool ideas and to ensure consistency of approach to dealing with domestic violence.

3. To raise the level of consciousness of police officers and of the public to the lonely and vulnerable plight of women subjected to violence in the home.

How can the Police Help?

First, a victim will be given the moral support of having someone who will listen sympathetically. A medical examination can be arranged, if necessary. The victim will then be advised about the various options which are open to him/her.

If the police are satisfied that a crime has been committed the abuser can be charged with that crime and tried in a criminal court. Domestic violence can also be dealt with under the civil law without charging the abuser with a criminal offence.

(a) Criminal proceedings

The victim will have any criminal proceedings explained to him/her. If necessary a police officer from the unit might attend court with the victim to give moral support. The officer would also keep the victim informed about what is happening with regard to court proceedings. For example, bail conditions might be imposed on a man who has assaulted his wife pending a full court hearing. Very often, those conditions would include a ban on his return home, for the protection of the wife. If the victim does not wish to take the matter to the criminal court, the domestic violence unit will keep a record of what has happened. If there is a further assault and the victim then decides that the matter must go to the criminal court, the record can help to show that there has been a pattern of violence.

(b) Civil law

Police officers will be able to refer victims to local solicitors who specialise in dealing with domestic violence in the civil courts.

Non-molestation Orders

A non-molestation order is made by the court to prevent your partner from using violence against you or from threatening you with violence, or from intimidating, harrassing, or pestering you. If that order is disobeyed by your partner he or she could be sent to prison. In some cases the court will not actually make an order, but will accept an undertaking instead. An undertaking is a solemn promise made to the court and has exactly the same effect, in that a breach of an undertaking may result in the person being sent to prison. This will always be explained very carefully by the judge to the person giving the undertaking.

CASE STUDY

Marie has been assaulted by her husband Reg. She goes to the county court to ask for an order protecting her from further violence. Reg denies that he has assaulted Marie. The court does not need to hear evidence from either Marie or Reg. The case is dealt with by the judge asking Reg if he is willing, without admitting that he has assaulted Marie in the past, to promise that he will not do so in the future. Reg agrees to do this, as it is pointed out to him that no finding is being made against him and he is making no admission of violence. The judge then explains to Reg that his promise to the court will be in the form of an undertaking, which Reg has to sign. Reg's undertaking is that he will not 'use or threaten to use violence' against Marie. The judge will explain very carefully to Reg that if he breaks that promise he risks being sent to prison.

In many cases, the fact that a man has had to appear before the court and give such a promise has the effect of making him realise for the first time how shameful his behaviour has been.

CASE STUDY

Lottie has been beaten up by her husband Max. She goes to the county court to get protection from him. Max denies that he has assaulted Lottie and claims that the injuries from which she suffered were the result of a fall downstairs. Max refuses to give undertakings and wants a full hearing by the court. Both Lottie and Max give evidence and the judge accepts Lottie's evidence. The judge can then make various different orders, according to the gravity of the assault and the other circumstances of the case. One order which will certainly be made is that Max should not use violence or threaten to use violence against Lottie.

If you have children, and there has been any violence or threat of violence to them, the court can include the children in the order. The order can cover any other matters which may be important in your particular case, for example your partner could be forbidden to telephone you or to loiter outside your place of work or the children's school.

Occupation Orders

The courts also have power to decide who should occupy your family home. If there has been serious violence and you do not feel that it is safe to continue living with your partner, or if you have actually left because of the violence and do not wish to return while he or she is still living there, you may want to apply for an occupation order. This will be an order that he or she leaves the home so that you can occupy it. Since ordering someone to leave his or her home is clearly a very serious matter, occupation orders are only granted when the court takes the view that the situation cannot be dealt with by non-molestation undertakings or orders.

Who can apply for an Occupation Order?

You must be an associated person to apply for an occupation order. Not every associated person is entitled to an order. If any of the following applies to you, you can apply.

1. You are the sole or joint tenant of your home, or are married to someone who is.

2. You are the owner or co-owner of your home, or are married to someone who is.

3. You have been married to the person who has a legal right to occupy the property.

4. You have lived as man and wife with the person who has a legal right to occupy the property.

Occupation orders can be granted for six months. In certain circumstances the period can be extended.

What should I do in an Emergency?

In an emergency you can always contact the Police by dialling 999.

Women's Aid have a national helpline [0345 023 468] which offers support, help and information to women who are experiencing, or who have experienced, domestic violence. If you need somewhere to stay or you need advice about legal matters, you will be able to talk to a volunteer in confidence. Even if all you need is someone to talk to about what is happening, you can talk for as long as you need and as often as you like.

Women's Aid also have about 250 refuges in the United Kingdom. These are safe houses which offer temporary accommodation for women and children who need to escape from domestic violence. You can be married or single, with or without children. The addresses and telephone numbers of refuges are secret, which makes it difficult for abusers to track their victims down. You can stay for a few days, a breathing space giving you a chance to think and make plans, or you might stay for several months. Women's Aid workers will help you to find accommodation if you need it.

If this is happening to you

If you are the victim of domestic violence, please remember:

(a) you are not alone, there are people who are willing to help;

(b) you are not to blame, the perpetrator is the one with the problem;

(c) you should contact the police, they will advise you of your options;

(d) the police will let you make your own decisions;

(e) the police will respect your confidentiality.

Useful Addresses

Women's Aid Federation (refuges for women and children)
PO Box 391
Bristol BS99 7WS
Telephone: 0117 944 4411
National Helpline: 0345 023 468

Alcoholics Anonymous
Telephone: 0171 8330022

London Rape Crisis Centre
PO Box 69
London WC1X 9N1
Telephone: 0171 837 1600

Men Overcoming Violent Emotions [MOVE]
32a Elmsmere Road
Didsbury M20 6FL
Telephone: 0161 434 7484

You could also try the Citizen's Advice Bureau [local directory].

SECTION V

PRACTICALITIES

CHAPTER FIFTEEN

GOING TO COURT

Most people find going to court to give evidence in a case a fairly scary experience – and this includes lawyers. I had to give evidence in court on one occasion and I was absolutely terrified. But this is not really surprising. If the hearing is in open court, all the trappings of the situation, the judge sitting above everyone in his/her formal robes, the wigs and gowns of the lawyers, even the ushers in their black gowns, all combine to make the atmosphere very formal and forbidding. The layout of the court itself, familiar from film and television sets, reinforces the solemnity. There may be members of the public there to watch the hearing; there may even be reporters from local or national papers, to make matters even worse.

It is your turn to be called to give your evidence. You have to make your way into the witness box, guided by the usher. You will be asked if you have a religion. If you are religious you will be given a copy of the Bible, the Koran or whatever is appropriate. The usher then hands you a card from which you read the words of an oath that you will tell the truth, the whole truth and nothing but the truth. Some people are so nervous that their tongues trip over the words. Others may have eyesight problems or may never have learned to read. If this happens the usher simply reads out the words of the oath which are repeated by the witness. If you have no religion you will be asked to affirm.

It is hardly surprising that the minds of many witnesses go blank in those first few seconds. Most people can't help panicking a little. Am I telling the truth?

CASE STUDY

Connie was struggling to give evidence in support of her divorce petition based on the unreasonable behaviour of her husband. She managed to give her name, her address and the date of her marriage. Then her barrister asked her what the problems in the marriage had been. The wife had suffered several beatings from her husband. She would have to give details about some of the occasions. They were all set out in the particulars of her petition. But she was so nervous that she could remember none of them.

There was a long silence. The barrister tried to help with another question. The difficulty for the barrister was that no 'leading question' can be asked in this situation. No question could be asked which suggested to the witness what the answer should be. The barrister could not ask whether the petitioner remembered the beating she had as a result of which she sustained a black eye and several bruises. 'Do you remember the night of the 24th June?' Connie said she did. 'What happened?' said the barrister encouragingly. Dead silence.

On this occasion, the judge did something rather unusual. He came down from the bench, walked round to the witness box, looked up at the tongue-tied petitioner and said, 'You know what he did, madam. Your barrister knows what he did. But the silly old judge doesn't know, and you have to tell him.'

That did the trick. But not every judge is quite so kind and compassionate, although most judges have sympathy with the feelings of witnesses who may be in court for the first time in their lives. They try to be as helpful as they can while keeping in mind that there are strict rules which have to be followed when evidence is given.

Thankfully, there is now no necessity for evidence to be given in the vast majority of divorce cases, where the whole matter can be dealt with on paper.

Although questions about children and financial matters relating to divorce are heard in court, the setting and atmosphere for such hearings are very much less formal than for defended divorce hearings. The judge and lawyers will not be wearing wigs and gowns. The hearings are in private, 'in chambers' is the legal expression. There will be a notice on the door, 'Court in Chambers', which means that no members of the public or reporters are permitted to be present in the court. Only the people directly concerned, who are parties to the proceedings, will be there with their legal advisers. Other people may be called as witnesses, but they will not be in court except when they are giving evidence.

Occasionally, when matters about children are being heard, a judge will give permission for stepfathers and stepmothers to be present in court throughout the hearing, in addition to the natural parents. The decision whether or not to allow anyone who is not a party to be present in court is one for the judge alone and the parties in the case will usually be asked whether or not they agree to those people being present before the judge makes his or her decision to allow them in.

Unmarried Partners

Disputes between unmarried partners about their children will also be heard in private. However, disputes about homes or other property between people who have not been married usually have to go to an open court hearing if the issues cannot be settled by agreement.

Before the Case

A lot of effort has gone into making courts more user-friendly recently. One result of this is that you will find that you can obtain a leaflet from most court buildings which will give you down to earth guidance on how your case will be dealt with. If you want to get hold of one of these leaflets you can ask for one at the court office between 10 am and 4 pm on any week day. If you have any questions – and who hasn't! – a member of the court staff will try to help. Court staff usually wear badges giving their names. If you can't get to the court yourself for any reason you can telephone to ask any questions between 9 am and 5 pm on any week day. You can also, of course, write to the court or send a fax. The address and telephone number of your county and magistrates' courts will be in your local telephone directory.

All documents relating to your case will have the name of the court at the top. There will also be a number in the top right-hand corner of the document. This is extremely important because court staff will always want to know the number of your case if you are asking any questions about it. Although court staff are not qualified to give legal advice, they will be able to supply names and addresses of local solicitors and advice agencies.

If You Need Special Help

If you are disabled and need help you should inform someone at the court office before coming to court. All courts make provision for access for disabled people, although the older courts will not have been purpose-built with this in mind.

You might be anxious about coming face to face with other people who are involved in your case while waiting for the case to be called on. If you are, you can ask if it would be possible for you to wait in some other area. Again, whether this will be possible obviously depends upon the facilities which the court has, but staff will always try to help.

If you do suffer from some disability, it is sensible to inform court staff in advance because it may at least be possible for them to ensure that you have the minimum waiting time before your case is called into court. The court building will have toilets and public telephones. Some courts have a cafeteria. In others the Women's Voluntary Service (WVS) may provide tea and coffee. Some have drinks vending machines – although it has to be said from experience that these seem to break down with depressing regularity!

How to Cope without a Lawyer

The government has recently made cuts in the availability of legal aid (see Chapter 16). This has meant that many more people are having to represent themselves at court hearings in family cases. Daunting as it may be to have to give evidence in court, presenting your own case without a lawyer to help you can be even more worrying. But there are a few simple ideas which may help.

Preparation

1. Cases about children

Make sure that you know exactly what you are going to ask for or what you are going to say in response to what the other person in the case is asking for. In most cases you will be asked to attend court for what is called a directions appointment. At this appointment there may be an order, if it is a case about children, that statements should be filed by a certain date. A statement simply sets out the facts about your case. You should always put the number of the case at the top right-hand corner of your statement. The name of the court and the names of the parties in the case – you and the person on the other side – should also be put at the top of your statement. The paragraphs and pages of a statement should be numbered so that everyone in court can quickly find any part of the statement about which questions may be asked.

This is how a statement in a case about a child might begin:

IN THE ....COURT   Case No ......

BETWEEN:

MARY X   Applicant

and

JOHN X   Respondent

1. I, Mary X ..... , of....... (address), make this statement in support of my application that ....I am the mother of Adam X........., who was born on .... The Respondent, John X ....is his father.

After setting out who everyone is, you should continue setting out the facts of your case and what you are saying about them in numbered paragraphs.

At the end of your statement you say in a final paragraph:

> I confirm that the contents of this statement are true to the best of my knowledge, information and belief and may be used in evidence.

Then you sign and date the statement, and take it to he court to be filed. The court will have given you a date by which the statements must be filed. If anyone else is going to give evidence on your side in the case, he or she should also make a statement in the same form.

You should send copies of all your statements to the person on the other side and, of course, keep copies for yourself. Cases about children are completely confidential, so you must not show any documents in the case to anyone who is not a party in the case or a legal adviser.

It almost goes without saying that you should never show a child any documents in a case about him or her. It is best, from the child's point of view, to involve him or her as little as possible in any dispute. Otherwise you put an unfair burden on the child, who will probably have very torn loyalties. The court welfare officer, or a guardian appointed to represent the child in the case, will be able to talk to the child about anything necessary in a neutral and sympathetic way.

2. *Cases about money or property*

If your case about family money or property is to be heard in the county court, directions will be given by the court about how the case is to proceed. The directions order might look like this.

IN THE......COUNTY COURT   Case No ......

BETWEEN:

MARY X   Applicant

and

JOHN X   Respondent

DIRECTIONS

1. The following directions shall apply to this application.

There will then follow numbered paragraphs, giving dates by which each of the parties has to file 'affidavit of means' and serve them on one another. An affidavit of means is a sworn document which sets out your income and your outgoings. You choose whether they are set out on a weekly, monthly or annual basis. But whichever you decide, please make sure that all the figures are on the basis you choose – it muddles everyone if you put weekly figures for some outgoings, monthly for others and annual figures for the rest!

An affidavit is headed in the same way as the 'directions order', and you set out the information in numbered paragraphs. You have to take it to a solicitor so that you can swear that the contents of the affidavit are true in his presence. The solicitor will charge a fee for the affidavit itself and for each exhibit to the affidavit. An exhibit is a document attached to your affidavit which you want to produce to the court – for example a bank statement or a wage slip.

The directions given by the court may include other matters. If there is a matrimonial home in dispute, for example, the court will direct that you and the other person must agree the value of the property. If you cannot agree, then each of you must obtain a valuation from an estate agent. At that stage, if the valuations are different, you ought to try to agree on a figure midway between the two. The alternative would be to bring the two estate agents to court to give evidence, and you would obviously have to pay them for their time which could be an unnecessary and expensive exercise.

Each case is different and this can only be the most general indication of what you can expect to have to do in a family dispute about money or property. Court staff will give you all the help they can, short of giving legal advice, if there is something which you do not understand. The directions order will always give the full address of the court.

On the Day of the Hearing

The court will have sent you a document giving the date and time at which your case will be heard. If for some reason that date and time are not convenient to you – for example, if you have a hospital appointment or are going to be away on holiday – make sure to get in touch with the court office immediately to let them know so that another date can be fixed. If anyone else is going to give evidence on your behalf, make sure that he or she knows about the date and can be there.

What to Wear

There are no rules about what you should wear in court. However. judges are human beings. They, and any lawyers appearing in the case, have to observe certain rules about how they should dress, as a mark of respect for the court. So it does not create a good impression it someone turns up for a hearing looking scruffy or wearing, for example, a rather sexy and obviously unsuitable dress. Wear clothes in which you feel comfortable and reasonably smart.

How to Address the Court

In a magistrates' court the magistrates are called 'sir' or 'madam'; district judges in county courts are also called 'sir' or 'madam'. County court judges are called 'your honour'. High court judges are called 'my lord' or 'my lady'. Do not worry unduly about what to call the judge, however. As long as you answer questions politely, the judge will not be concerned if you get the title wrong. Even lawyers get mixed up sometimes.

Timing

It is a help to arrive at court in good time, especially if you are being represented by a barrister who may not have met you before. Although he or she will know all about your case because they will have been given full details by your solicitor, it is important to have a discussion before the case starts. Most courts open at 9.30 am, although there are some which do not open to the public until 10 am. The hours will be displayed on a notice board outside the court or the court staff can give you the information.

On your Arrival

When you arrive tell the receptionist or the court usher, who will be wearing a black gown and carrying a clipboard with a list of cases.

There will probably be more than one court in the building, each having its own number. Find out under which court number your case has been listed. If a solicitor or barrister is representing you, he or she will want to have a discussion about aspects of the case (called a conference) before the hearing. Your barrister is not allowed to discuss the case with any of your witnesses, and so may ask them to stay outside the room where you are having your discussion, or out of earshot if there is no room available. This is because there must be no suggestion that your barrister has influenced what one of the witnesses might say.

The hearing will never start before the time which has been given to you. However, it is not at all certain that it will start on time. Often you will find that several cases have been listed to start at the same time. This is not as contrary as it sounds, because court staff have to allow for the fact that settlements of disputes are often negotiated outside the door of the court, so some of the cases may need time for discussion. If one of the cases is settled by agreement, the hearing before the judge will obviously be very short, just sufficient time for the judge to be told what agreement has been reached and to be invited to approve it.

When your case is called into court try not to feel too nervous, especially if you have no lawyer to help you. The judge will tell you when it is your turn to ask questions of other witnesses or to give evidence yourself. Never interrupt when you have not been told it is your turn to speak. Your turn will come and the judge will listen to you with patience and attention.

Evidence

Your statements or affidavits are part of your evidence. You do not need to tell the judge about anything which you have already included in one of those documents, because he or she will already have read them. There may be other things which you would like to add when you get into the witness box. The judge will allow you to do this.

Speak clearly and in a voice which is loud enough for everyone in court to hear what you are saying. Try not to go too fast, the judge will probably be trying to write everything down. A good tip is to watch the judge's pen while you give evidence. Pause until he catches up with you and stops writing.

If there are any documents which you wish the judge to read, you should have provided copies of them to the other side before the hearing. It is an excellent idea to make three photocopies of all documents which you are going to use in court, so that there will be a copy for the judge, a copy for the other side and a copy for you. If there are a large number of documents, put the copies in three bundles in the same order, with the same page numbers in each bundle. This will mean that everyone will be able to find any of the documents quickly. Make a written list of any questions which you want to ask each of the witnesses who will be giving evidence before you come to court. This helps to ensure that you do not forget anything.

You do not have to use legal language. Just say what you mean, in as few words as you can. If you do not understand something which is said, do not be afraid to say so and ask what it means.

If you are giving evidence yourself when the court adjourns (stops for lunch or overnight or any other break), remember that there is a strict rule that you are not allowed to discuss the case or your evidence with anyone during the period for which you are not in court. This includes your lawyer, so don't be surprised if he or she walks away if you try to speak outside court.

When you are Asking Questions

Trial scenes in films and television programmes often give the impression that cross examination should be conducted in an aggressive and unpleasant manner. This could not be more unfortunate from the point of view of family cases.

Family judges will very speedily become irritated and displeased when anyone attempts to bully or intimidate a witness in a family case. It is much more sensible – and effective – to ask questions in a pleasant and friendly manner. Lawyers who specialise in family work rarely subject witnesses to the abrasive type of cross examination frequently seen in the criminal courts. If they attempt to do so, they are likely to find themselves being quickly rebuked by the judge.

Equally, when you are being cross examined, it is much more effective to keep your replies polite – and as short as you can. Avoid asking questions in return: 'How would you like to find your wife with another man?' is not a response which is going to find favour with the judge.

Keep as calm as you can when you are in court. It is difficult to sit quietly while someone is giving evidence which you might find hurtful and downright untruthful. The temptation to interrupt is sometimes very strong. But remember that judges are highly experienced in listening to evidence. Lies or exaggeration are quickly detected by them. Giving vent to your emotion will certainly not help, and may indeed be to your disadvantage.

People rarely seem to realise that a judge is very much aware of everything which goes on in the court – one of the reasons why he or she usually sits in an elevated seat. Observing the reactions of parties listening to others giving evidence can be part of the judge's overall assessment of the case. So it is not just when you are in the witness box that your behaviour is important.

People who snigger or sneer when evidence is being given are not giving their own case the best chance possible. This is worth remembering whether you are representing yourself or being represented. Your lawyer will often be sitting in front of you, so will be unaware of how you may be reacting, but the judge will be very much aware of everything which is going on.

CHAPTER 16

LEGAL COSTS

Taking a case to court is a very expensive business. This is one of the reasons for thinking very carefully indeed about whether you actually need to fight over children, money or the matrimonial home when your marriage or relationship breaks down. If it is at all possible to come to an agreement between yourselves about what should happen, you can save yourselves a great deal of expense, not to mention a considerable amount of emotional stress. This is where skilled mediation can help, and it costs very much less than employing lawyers.

But there are cases where there is no hope of agreement. So how do you go about finding a solicitor to advise you about your case? Not all firms of solicitors advise in family matters. The Solicitors Family Law Association (address and telephone number at the end of this chapter) will be able to inform you of those who specialise in family cases in your area.

Another helpful source of information about local solicitors who specialise in family law will be your local Citizen's Advice Bureau (address in telephone directory). Friends or relatives who have used a solicitor in their own family case might be able to recommend someone.

If you are Paying Yourself

People are often worried about going to see a solicitor in case they find themselves facing an enormous bill straight away. But many solicitors in fact charge little or nothing for the first interview. Each solicitor has an hourly rate and will charge on the basis of the number of hours spent on a case. In the London area, the minimum hourly charge would be about £80, the maximum could be several hundreds. A sensible first step when you make an appointment to see a solicitor is to find out what the hourly charge is going to be.

Remember that every letter written and every telephone call made by your solicitor on your behalf will have to be charged for – it's rather like a taxi meter running all the time. Your solicitor should inform you of the likely costs before starting any work for you, and should also keep you up to date on how much your case is costing. You will probably be asked to pay some money on account at your first meeting, and then be asked to top that up with more payments on account as the case proceeds.

If your case becomes complicated or prolonged, if you are battling over money and the matrimonial home for example, the costs can run into thousands of pounds, particularly if there has to be a court hearing.

The First Interview

An appointment with a solicitor can be made by telephone or by calling at the office. Explain briefly what your case is about when you make the appointment. That should ensure that you see the right person, because it is unlikely that everyone in the particular firm you have chosen will specialise in family law. Unless it is very urgent, you should usually be offered an appointment within five working days. If it would be difficult for you to travel to the office, perhaps because you are disabled in some way, ask if it would be possible for someone to see you at home.

Because solicitors do have to charge by the hour, it makes sense to concentrate on making the most of the time as possible. A little preparation can be a great help. First, be clear about the points you want to get across and the information which you need from the solicitor. A written list of the questions you want to ask and reminders of points you want to make is a good idea.

Collect together all the letters and other papers which you may have in connection with the case so that you have them ready to bring to the interview.

At the interview the solicitor will ask you a lot of questions and make notes of your answers. He or she will be anxious to help. If you have questions, ask them. If the solicitor uses some legal word which is unfamiliar, ask what it means.

At the end of the meeting ask your solicitor to write to you confirming:

(a) that he or she has taken on the work;

(b) what advice you have been given;

(c) the name of the person in the firm who will be dealing with your case;

(d) the time everything is likely to take;

(e) when you will next hear from your solicitor;

(f) what the costs are likely to be in your case;

(g) whether the solicitor needs any more information from you;

(h) the name of the person in the firm to contact should you have any complaint about your solicitor's services

Keeping in Touch

It is important to keep in regular contact with your solicitor. You should be consulted at every stage of the case about what is to happen. But do remember that it keeps the costs down if you avoid unnecessary telephone calls or correspondence with your solicitor. You should always ask when you may next expect to hear from your solicitor. If you do not hear anything by the promised date, you are entitled to ask why and to request a progress report.

Changing your Solicitor

If you are paying your solicitor yourself, and you are unhappy about the way he is handling your case for some reason, you can change to another firm of solicitors at any time. It would be usual in those circumstances for your original solicitor to ask that all his fees be paid before he releases his file on the case to the new solicitor. If you have paid the full fees, your original solicitor must hand over the file.

If you are legally aided you need permission from your legal aid area office to change solicitors. You have to explain why you wish to change. For example, you might have moved house and wish to change to a firm in your new locality.

If your firm of solicitors decides to transfer your case to someone else in the firm, they should tell you at once. If you are not happy with the change, you can take the case to a new solicitor (again with the permission of the legal aid area board if you are legally aided).

The National Consumer Council publish a helpful leaflet called *Getting the Best from your Solicitor*, copies of which can be obtained from your local Citizen's Advice Bureau or law centre (addresses in telephone directory).

Legal Aid

Solicitors who take legally aided cases usually display the legal aid logo prominently outside their offices. The Law Society (address and telephone number at the end of this chapter) will provide you with names of legal aid solicitors in your area. At your first appointment, the solicitor has a duty to advise you if he or she thinks that you are eligible for legal aid. If that particular solicitor does not accept clients who are legally aided, he or she should still point out that you are entitled to it and would probably tell you the names of local firms who take legally aided cases.

Green Form Cases

If you earn less than a certain amount a week net and have a limited amount of capital, you are entitled to green form legal aid. The amounts vary from time to time, but your solicitor will be able to tell you what they are. In this type of legal aid, you would be offered advice and assistance but not representation in court proceedings. The only exception to this is that green form legal aid will cover undefended divorce proceedings.

If you are the petitioner in the divorce, your green form will cover three hours' free advice and assistance from your solicitor. This does not mean that you would actually spend three hours with the solicitor, as it includes time spent on, for example, letter writing, or steps taken in divorce proceedings. If you are the respondent in the divorce, your green form only covers two hours of free advice and assistance.

Your disposable income will be calculated after deducting income tax, national insurance and allowances for any dependants you have. If, after those calculations have been made, you have income and capital which are lower than the current limits then you will be eligible for green form legal aid. If you are in receipt of family credit, are on income support or are receiving a disability allowance, you will be entitled to it.

If all this sounds complicated, remember that a solicitor can help you to work out whether or not you will be entitled. When calculating your capital assets in a divorce case, any capital assets which are in dispute between you and your spouse – for example, your matrimonial home, other possessions or money – will not be taken into account when assessing your entitlement to legal aid.

Legal Aid Certificate

This is the second type of legal aid. It covers representation wherever there are disputes in court about children or finances, but it will not cover undefended divorce proceedings. A legal aid certificate can be granted to cover a defended divorce, but this would be very unusual.

The financial limits for obtaining a legal aid certificate are more generous than those for getting legal aid under the green form scheme. Costs of housing and the repayment of debts can be taken into account when calculating net income. Again, your solicitor will be able to help you decide whether you would be entitled to a legal aid certificate. You may be asked to make a monthly payment, depending on your income.

If you have been granted a legal aid certificate, you have a continuing obligation to tell the legal aid board about any change in your financial situation – for example, if you get a rise in salary, a better-paid job or a win on the pools. If you do not notify the board of such changes, your certificate could be discharged or revoked. If it is revoked, you would have to pay back any costs which have already been met by legal aid.

Have you got a Good Case?

The financial test is not the only one which you have to pass in order to obtain legal aid, you also have to satisfy the legal aid board that you have reasonable grounds to take or to defend the proceedings. Sometimes your legal aid certificate could be limited to obtaining counsel's opinion on the merits of your case. This simply means that your solicitor will ask a barrister who specialises in family law to give a written opinion that you are more than likely to succeed if the case goes ahead.

Your solicitor must also tell the legal aid board if he thinks you are being unreasonable about your case. If you were involved in a dispute about money, and your spouse made an offer to settle which your solicitor believed could not be bettered as the result of a court hearing, it would then be the duty of the solicitor to inform the legal aid board and your legal aid certificate could be discharged.

Paying your Legal Aid Back

If you recover or preserve – that is to say get or keep – any money or property (including the matrimonial home) as a result of your case, the legal aid board have to be repaid costs which have been paid by the legal aid fund, if the total which you get or keep is over £2,500. In matrimonial proceedings, if you do not get or keep more than £2,500, you do not have to repay the legal aid board.

In many cases the ex-wife or husband is given the matrimonial home as a result of the proceedings. There may be children living there. To avoid someone in that position having to sell their home in order to meet the debt for legal aid, it is possible to arrange for the debt to be a charge, the same as a mortgage, on the property. This means that the debt does not have to be paid until the property is sold. In some cases the court can direct that the charge should be transferred to another property when the matrimonial home is sold. Interest will be charged on the amount owing to the legal aid board until the debt is paid.

If the court has ordered that your ex must pay your costs, then your debt to the legal aid board will be reduced by the amount of costs paid under the order. But even if you get an order for costs, you will usually find that the costs actually paid do not cover all the costs which have arisen. Correspondence between your solicitor and the legal aid board, for example, is not something for which the other side would be expected to pay under a costs order.

Useful Addresses

National Consumer's Council
20 Grosvenor Gardens
LondonSW1W ODH
Telephone: 0171 730 3469

Solicitors Family Law Association (SFLA)
PO Box 302
Keston
Kent BR2 61TZ
Telephone: 0689 85022

Law Society
113 Chancery Lane
London WC2A 1PL
Telephone: 0171 242 1222

Legal Aid (for leaflets and enquiries)
Information Section
85 Grays Inn Road
London WC1X 8AA

GLOSSARY

Abduction of child: wrongful removal of child.

Access order: now called a contact order.

Acknowledgment of service: document in which a respondent (and co-respondent if any) acknowledges that the petition has been received.

Adultery: sexual intercourse between a married person and someone of the opposite sex.

Affidavit: a written statement to be used in court the truth of which has been sworn or affirmed by the person making it.

Ancillary: incidental or attached to – ancillary relief describes the orders which the court can make about money or property which are incidental to divorce or judicial separation proceedings.

Answer: a defence to a petition by the other spouse (called the respondent).

Application: a document which sets out what the court is being asked to do.

Care and control: an order made before the Children Act 1989 which gave someone (usually a parent) the day-to-day responsibility for looking after a child; these orders have been replaced by residence orders.

Care order: an order committing a child to the care of a local authority.

Chambers: most cases about children or financial matters are heard in Chambers – no one is allowed in court unless directly concerned with the case.

Charge: like a mortgage on property – when the property is sold the holder of the charge (e.g. the other spouse or the legal aid fund) must be paid the amount of the charge

Child of the family: any child of petitioner and respondent or any child they have treated as theirs (but not fostered children)

Child support: maintenance paid by parent with whom child does not live.

Child Support Agency (CSA): government agency set up for assessment, collection and enforcement of maintenance to be paid by "absent" (i.e. non-residential) parents

Conciliation: does not mean reconciliation – an attempt to help divorcing or separating partners to reach agreements when there are arguments about children or money.

Consent order: a court order which sets out what has been agreed.

Contact: used to be called access – a contact order sets out periods and/or dates when someone (usually a parent) may visit a child, have the child to stay, write to or telephone the child

Contempt of court: disobedience to an order of the court punishable by fine or imprisonment

Co-respondent: the person with whom it is alleged that the respondent has committed adultery.

Costs: an order that one party pays all or some of the legal costs of the other.

Counsel: barrister.

Court welfare officer: appointed by court to investigate and report on a dispute about a child.

Cross decrees: where the petitioner obtains a decree on the petition and the respondent on the answer.

Cross petition: where the respondent claims that the marriage has broken down because of the petitioner's behaviour.

Custody: an order made before the Children Act 1989 giving one or both parents the right to make decisions about a child, now replaced by joint parental responsibility, residence and contact orders.

Decree absolute: the final order which dissolves the marriage

Decree nisi: document certifying that the court is satisfied that there are grounds for a divorce – allows the petitioner to apply for decree absolute after six weeks

Directions: orders made by the court about how the case is to proceed – e.g. for the filing of evidence.

Disclosure: providing information to the court and the other side.

Exhibit: a document which is referred to in and attached to a sworn affidavit.

Ex parte: an application made to a court without giving the other side notice.

Filing: leaving documents with the court office.

Green form: legal aid scheme for limited amount of advice and help.

Guardian: someone glen parental responsibility for a child.

Guardian ad litem: someone appointed to act for a child in a court case.

Injunction: court order telling someone what to do or forbidding someone from doing something (e.g. where there has been domestic violence).

Legal aid: government assistance with legal costs.

Non-molestation: an injunction order forbidding someone to assault, pester, threaten or interfere with another person or persons.

Notice of application: court form on which an application is made setting out what is being asked for.

Ouster: injunction order which excludes someone from his or her home.

Parental responsibility: primarily the duties which a parent has to a child but also incorporating rights – a mother and the father married to her at date of conception or pregnancy have it automatically.

Penal notice: a warning on a court order that disobedience to it could mean committal to prison.

Petition: the document which asks the court for a decree of divorce or judicial separation.

Petitioner: the wife or husband who starts divorce proceedings by filing a petition.

Prohibited steps order: made under the Children Act to forbid a parent from doing something (e.g. taking the child abroad).

Questionnaire: list of questions asking for further information about financial matters.

Reciprocal enforcement: when two countries have agreed to enforce the orders made by one another's courts.

Recovered or preserved: money, or property which has been gained or kept in the course of legal proceedings.

Relevant child: child of the family who is not yet sixteen at date of decree nisi or who is still in full-time education or training, or is disabled or dependent.

Reply: document filed by petitioner in response to answer and/or cross petition.

Reserved costs: where court postpones decision on costs until a later hearing of the case.

Residence order: made under the Children Act 1989 to direct where a child will live – only necessary where there is disagreement.

Respondent: the husband or wife who does not file the petition.

Service: giving copies of documents to the other side – some need to be served personally, others by post, some by you and some by the court – the court office will explain.

Special procedure: where the divorce is undefended (no answer filed by the respondent) there is normally no need to appear in court and a copy of the decree nisi is sent to husband and wife by the court.

Specific issue order: an order under the Children Act 1989 which decides some dispute about a child – e.g. where he or she should go to school.

Spouse: a husband or a wife.

Statement of arrangements: a form which has to be filed with a petition if there are any relevant children – it sets out the proposed arrangements for the children.

Statutory charge: the amount which has to be paid to the legal aid fund out of any money or property which has been recovered or preserved in the case.

Subpoena: an order requiring that someone comes to a court hearing.

Summons: an order that someone attends court at a specified time or date.

Undefended divorce: where the respondent does not oppose the divorce being granted.

Undertaking: a solemn promise to the court to do or not to do something; it has the same effect as an order, which means that a person giving an undertaking risks going to prison if he or she breaks the promise.

Without prejudice: anything said or written without prejudice during negotiations cannot be disclosed to the court if no agreement is reached.

INDEX